Match Fishing

FISHING STEP BY STEP

Match Fishing

with

Ray Mumford

CASSELL
LONDON

CASSELL & COMPANY LIMITED
35 Red Lion Square, London WC1R 4SG
and at Sydney, Auckland, Toronto, Johannesburg,
an affiliate of
Macmillan Publishing Co., Inc.,
New York.

First published 1976

ISBN 0 304 29749 6

Printed by Ian Allan Printing Ltd.

INTRODUCTION

If you can put a rod together, use a reel and handle a landing net, then these books are your next need. With this series of books the angler is given the chance of seeing just how the expert goes about catching the fish that have made his name a household word in the world of fishing.

Peter Mohan has used his unique knowledge of angling personalities to select the right angler for each book, and then edited the series as a whole.

Ken Whitehead has spent days at the water with the experts, patiently filming and planning every photograph so that each picture shows in detail where, when and how the many tasks are approached.

Study the pictures and compare your methods, your tackle and your whole approach to fishing. This is how you will gain the confidence that brings success.

Whilst the books in themselves are interesting to read, they are also a programmed technique that is progressive. With careful study the new angler, or one wishing to improve his angling will learn how each skill at the water should be tackled, and by re-reading he will be able to adopt the expert's way of tackling every situation.

1

1 There are no gimmicks in successful match fishing, and no short cuts. Just lots of hard work. By the time I get to this stage, putting my tackle in the van before leaving for the match, half of the job is done. My van is kept especially for fishing, and into it go

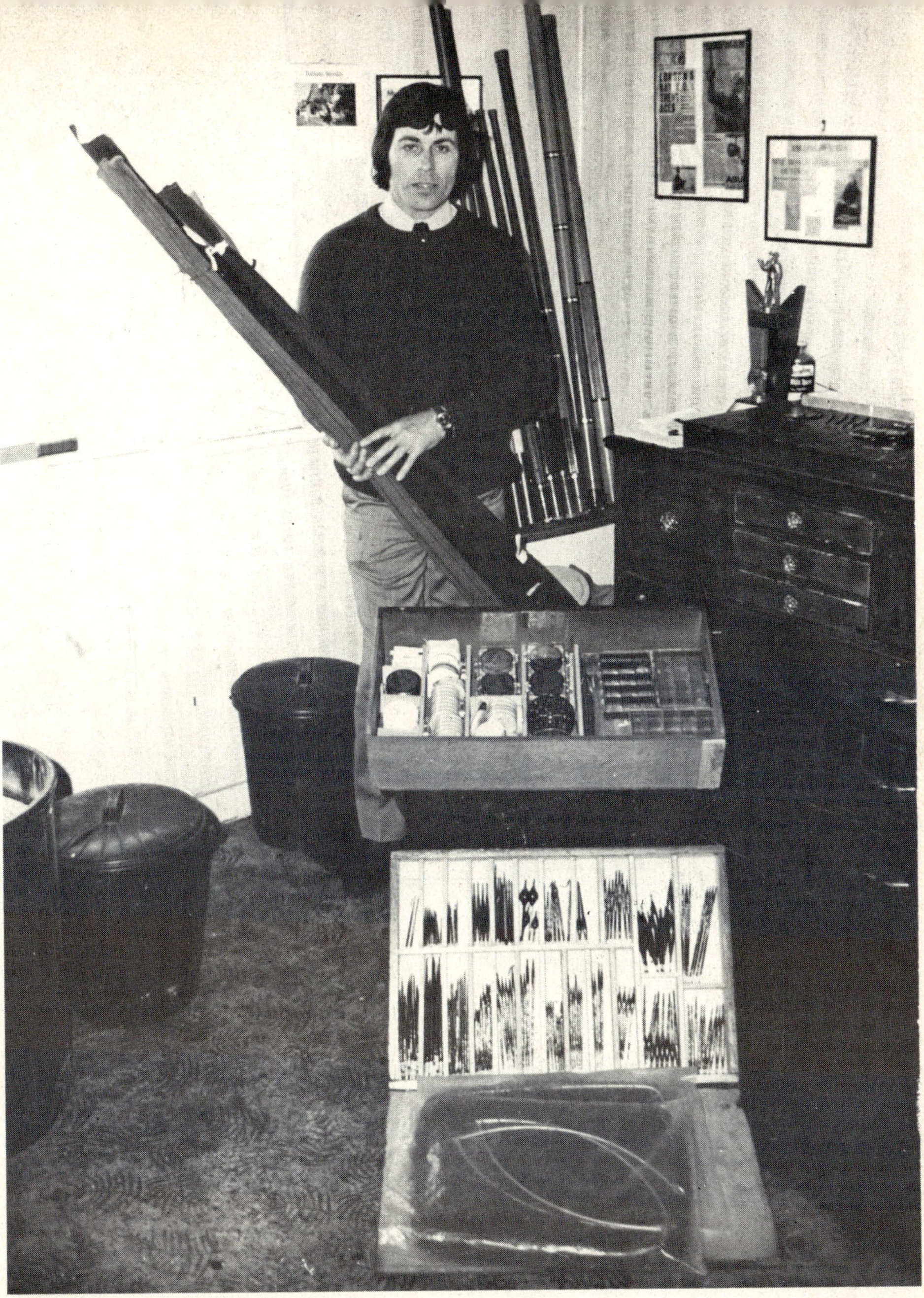

2

my rods in special partitions set in the roof where they won't get damaged. My other gear includes food, drink and spare equipment.

2 This room in my flat is set aside for fishing gear. Down the walls I hang rods, each in their bag, and in various chests I store spare tackle.

GROUND BAIT
BCM
BRITISH GROUNDBAITS,
BARDFIELD SALING, Nr. BRAINTREE
ESSEX

4

3 Not only my tackle but baits are kept here, in bulk, so that I can suit any water I am going to fish with a groundbait or hookbait that I know will be as near perfection as possible.

4 A good set of sieves is essential in bait preparation. My own are home-made, and besides separating maggots, etc,I use them with cereal baits to rid them of impurities, and to ensure even texture.

3

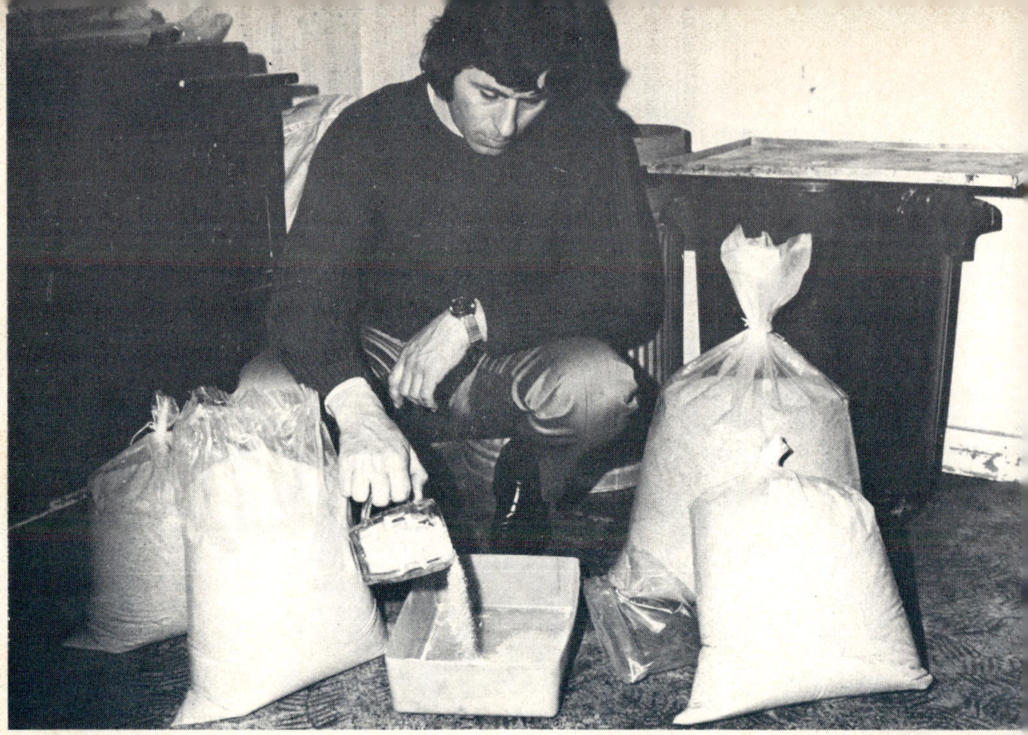

5

6

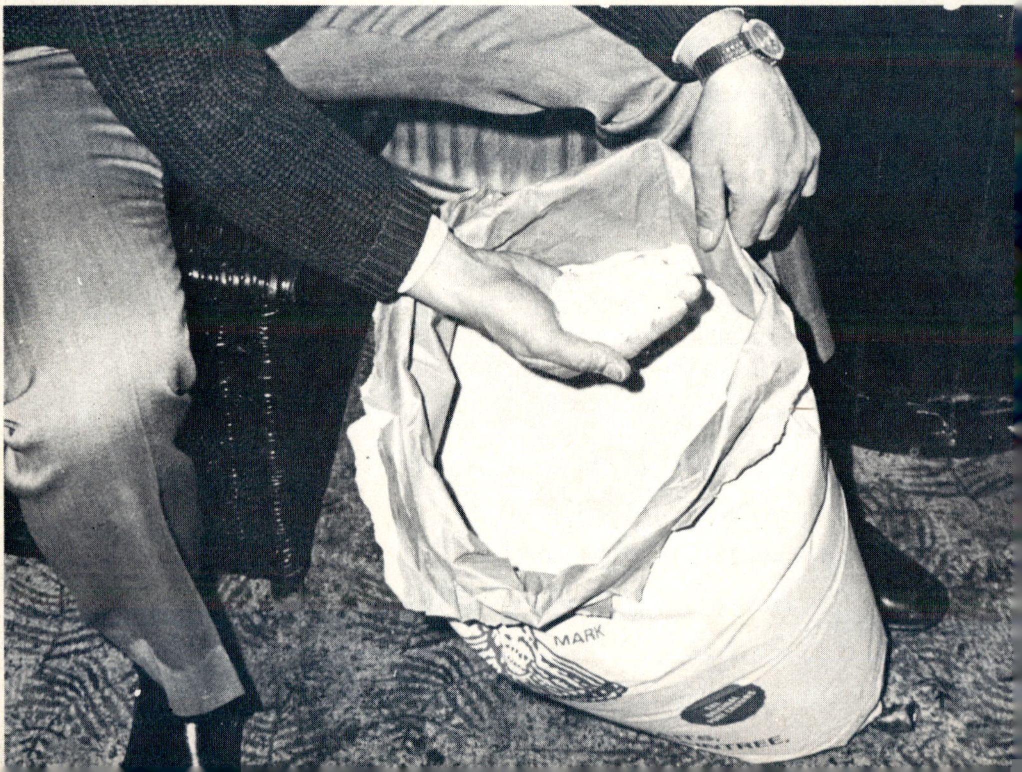

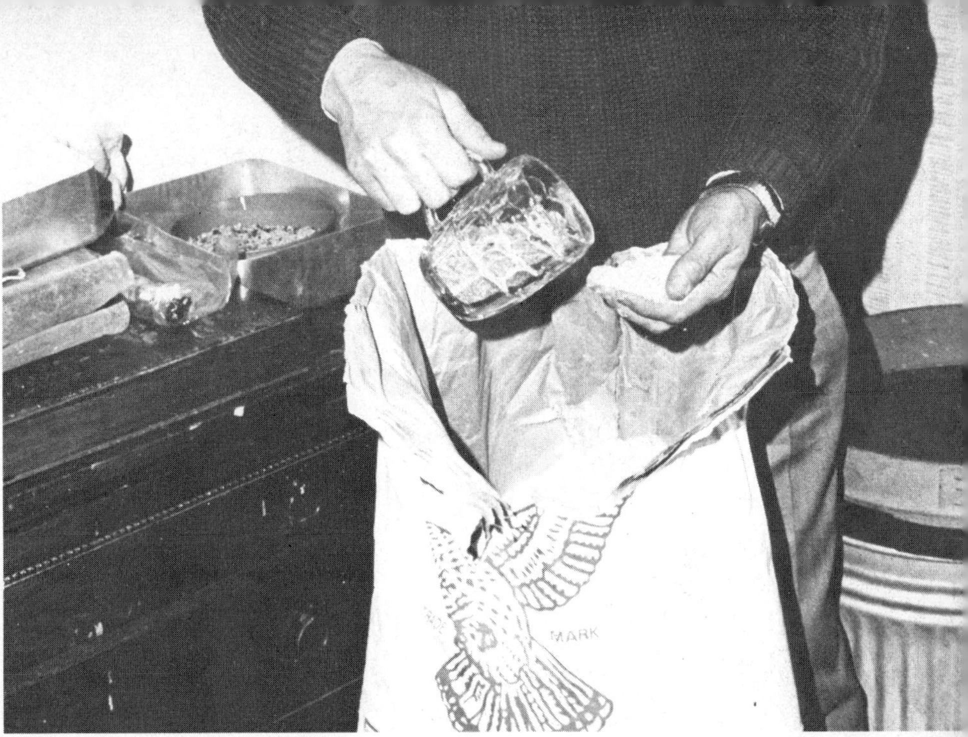

5 There is no such thing as a 'secret' groundbait. The only successful groundbait is one prepared the night before going to the match, from a fresh stock, and blended to suit the situation — heavy for fast, light for slow waters.

6 Breadcrumbs are the basis of most groundbaits, and because of the amount I use I find it cheaper to buy in 1cwt lots.

7 Bran is lighter than breadcrumbs, and also cheaper. Again it is cheaper in bulk — but must be kept dry.

8

9

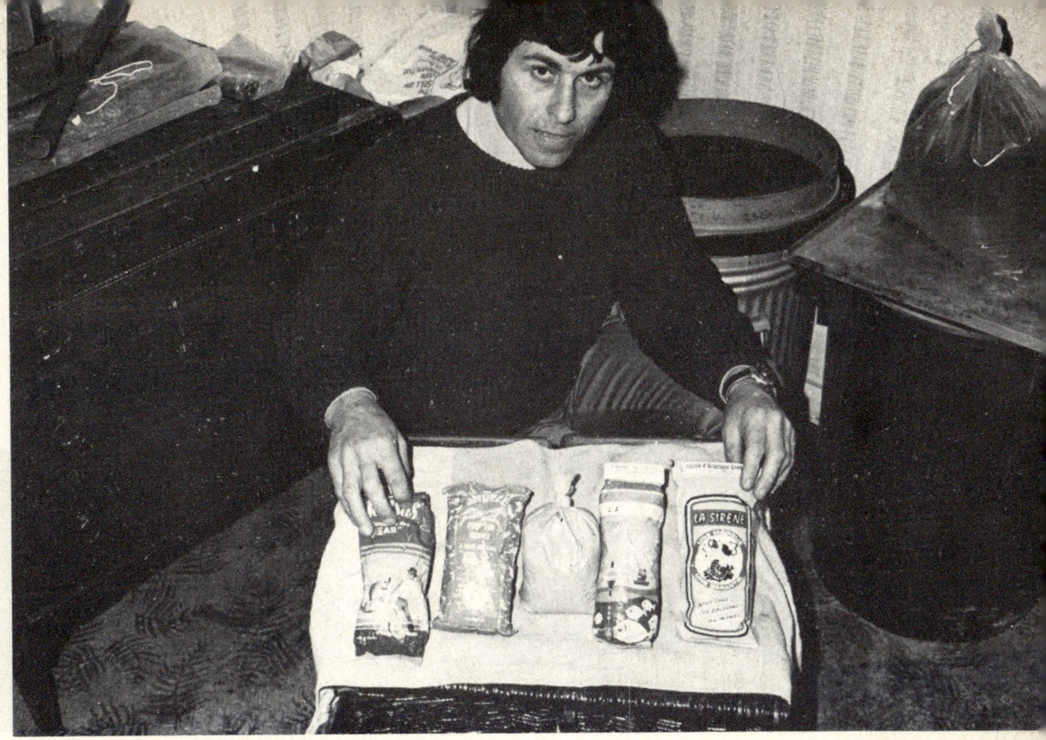

10

8 Biscuit meal, excellent 'bulk' feed for heavy water, is stored in a dustbin to stop it from crushing into dust. It must be kept bone-dry before use.

9 To darken groundbait there is nothing to beat a little dried blood. I buy this in small amounts and mix it with the bulk before I leave for the water.

10 Whilst on my many trips to the continent I was introduced to French groundbaits. These are pre-packed, very light in texture, and excellent for a 'cloud' effect. Their main disadvantage is expense — but fortunately a little goes a long way.

11

12

11 Maggots are the mainstay of the match angler. I will if occasion demands rear my own, but I buy the vast majority I use, paying a fair price and getting a good bait in return. Naturally, all maggots bought have to be worked on before use.

12 The first task after getting maggots home is to sieve them, ridding them of old husks and roughage that has been used as packing.

13 After careful sieving they are mixed with bran, to clean them further and keep the skins soft.

14

15

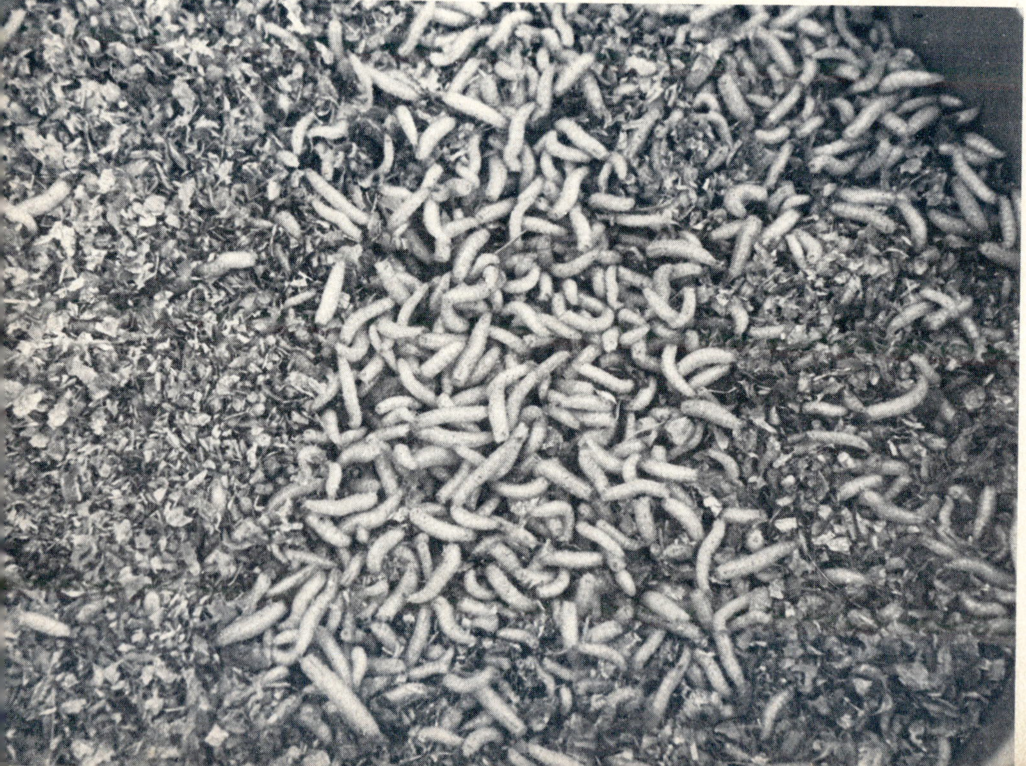

14 Finally, they are kept in escape-proof trays in the fridge until just before I set out. This stops them turning into casters.

15 Pinkies are small maggots, and I use them principally for groundbait, or as a 'switch' bait if fish are very shy. They are prepared in the same way.

16 To avoid confusion, here is a picture of pinkies and maggots together, and the difference in size can easily be seen.

Wilson w
speak abo
land deal
Have you ever seen a line of bank notes 2½ miles long?
EXCLUSIVE: The REAL Jane Fonda story

17

18

17 When fish will not take the ordinary maggots, they can often be tempted with red, orange or brown dyed specials. Here they are being dyed with a proprietary brand of maggot dye, following the maker's instructions.

18 Casters are useful as a hookbait. It is well worth the effort of producing your own.

19 Keep a pint of maggots warm, and as they start to turn into casters sieve them carefully. Keep them separate.

20

21

20 Sieve daily and store in the fridge until there are no further maggots to turn.

21 At the final separation sort through and remove debris, and dried-out shells.

22 Once stored in a polythene bag they will keep in the fridge until required. Remember, this is a task that takes several days — don't leave it until the night before the match.

23 Of course, I use many other baits — hempseed for example. The cheapest will do for crushing, which makes it go further as groundbait. But that for use on the hook must be the very best, cooked until the white kernel just shows, and kept damp throughout the day so that it will sink.

22

23

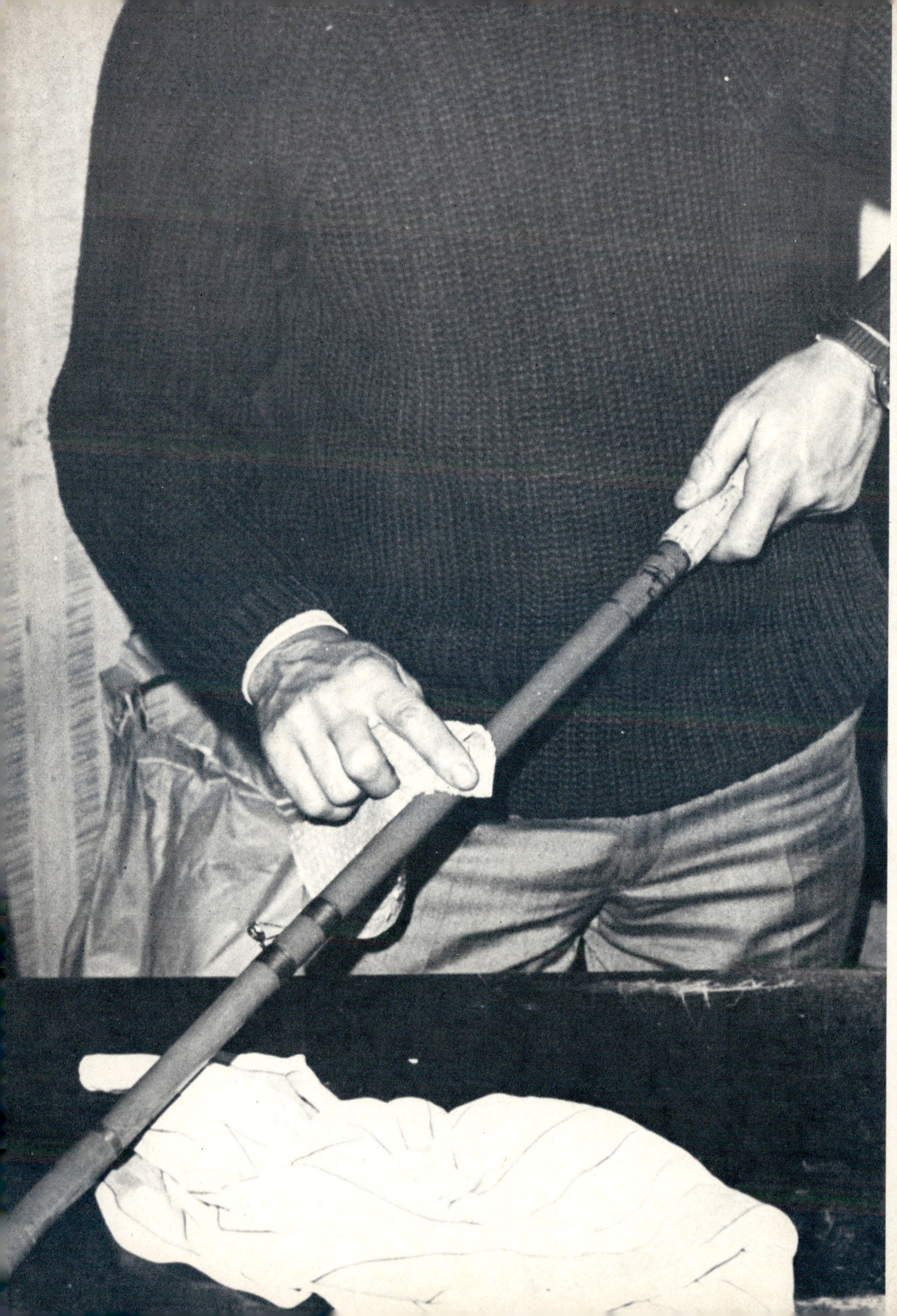

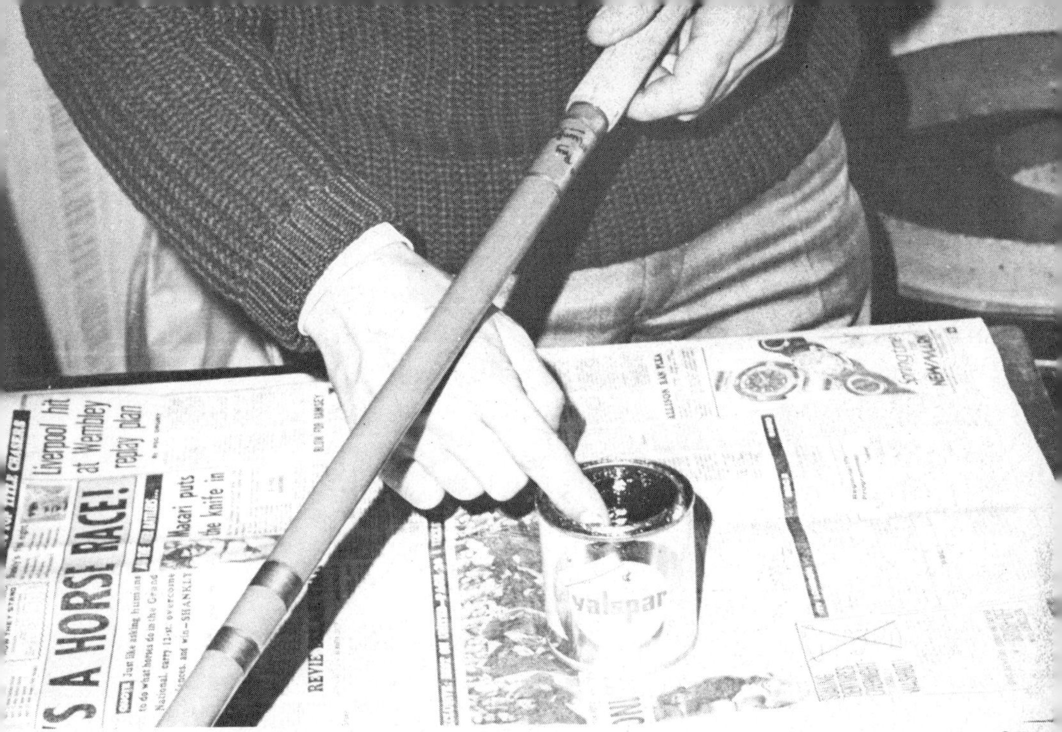

25

24 I find that clean tackle gives me confidence — it is a constant reminder that I have the best available. It takes minutes only after an outing to oil reels, clean rods and handles, and tidy small items of tackle.

25 Repairs and maintenance are necessary stages not only during the close season, but during the height of the fishing year. If a rod needs a lick of varnish, or a ring needs re-whipping — do it immediately. Then it can't let you down.

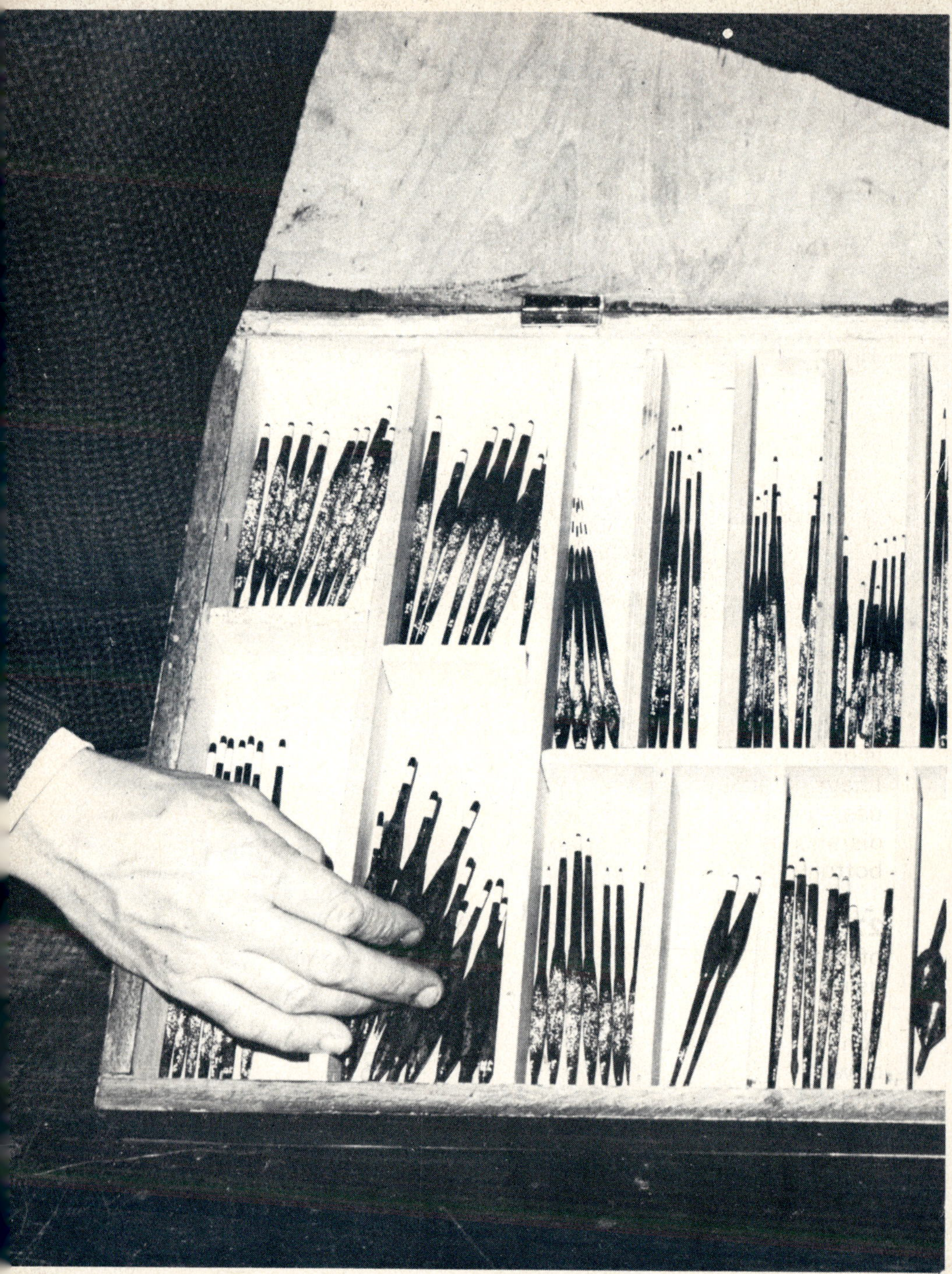

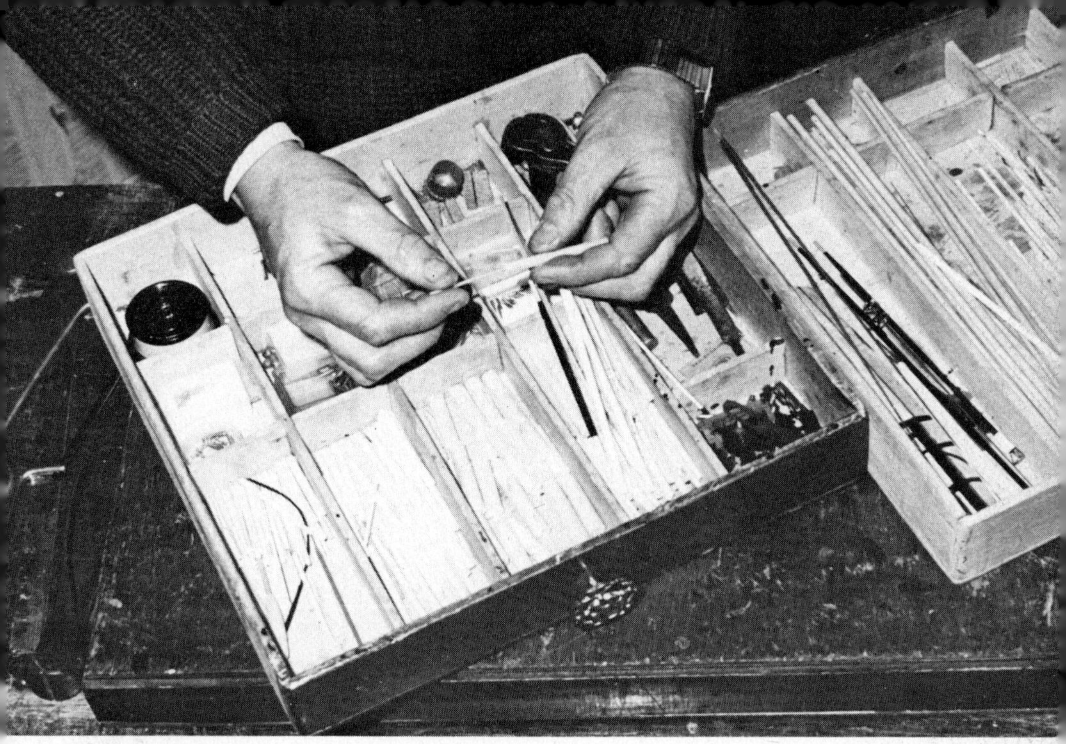

26 A float is the halfway mark between the angler and a fish. It must tell the angler everything that is going on — and the fish nothing. I have over 500, and each has a use, dependent on wind, water, distance to be cast, bait, and bottom.

27 To give me such a wide range of choice in floats I make my own, using practically every material imaginable and experimenting constantly. I have on occasions sat down the night before the match and made what I wanted for the next day.

28

28 Now for some practical work at the water. If I am fishing a pegged-down match, I just have to grin and bear the luck of the draw like everyone else. But don't give up a swim just because it looks bad. Search the water in front of you, study the banks and try to imagine the shape of the river bed. Decide on how you are going to fish it and be prepared, perhaps even after five minutes, to change styles and perhaps go on changing until you hit the fish.

29 The roving match really gives you a fighting chance to use your skill and find the right swim. But be prepared for a walk — unless you have been lucky enough to fish the water within a few days of the competition, in which case you will have definite ideas on which section to make for.

30 Only years of experience will tell you the good points of a swim. Here I chose the swim because there was a good 'draw' on the water, there appeared to be a good depth — something I learned by watching the course boats were taking — and the bed is gravel, seen at the water's edge. There is some weed and a high bank behind me for cover. Bushes on either side give some privacy.

31 Carrying an armful of rods will ensure you arrive at the swim exhausted. That is why I have a strong rod holdall, with a wide shoulder strap to prevent it rubbing the shoulders.

32 My three piece trotting rod is an all-round 13ft model that is light, but strong and sensitive enough to handle a small gudgeon or big barbel. No special tapers, no fancy fittings — just reliability.

33 The roachpoles I use are all ferruled, and not telescopic. I find them more sensitive, and even though they are more expensive I find them well worth the money. None of them has a black finish.

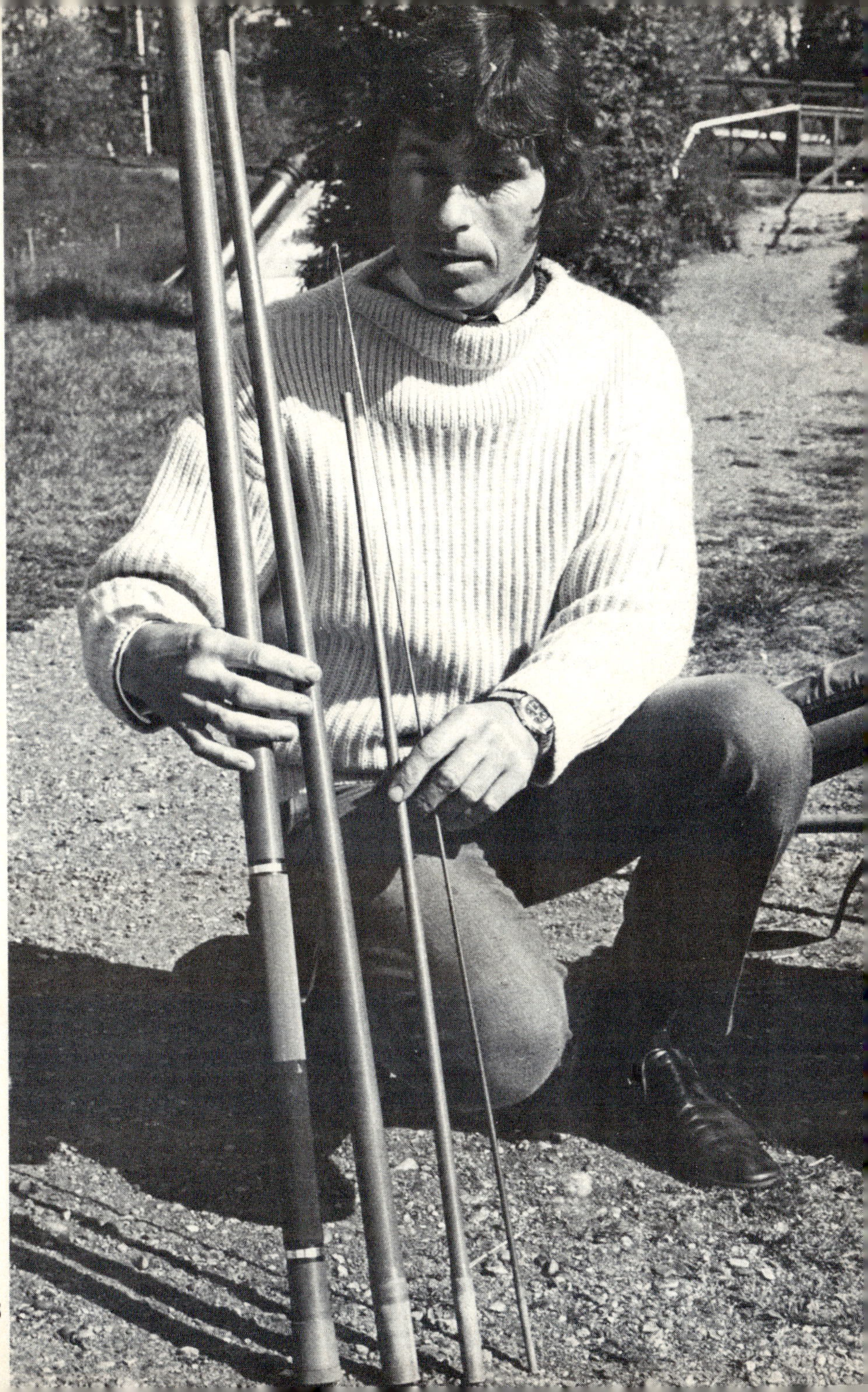

34

34 I carry a range of poles from 2 metres to 8 metres, not because of the risk of breakage but to enable me to cover a wide range of water, from that at my feet to near mid-stream.

35 This ledger rod is 8ft 6in long, and I made it to be a good all-round weapon capable of sensitive tip work, or heavy block-end casting.

37

36 A few of the rods carried for a competition. In all I carry ten — not for show, or to guard against breakage, but to make sure that I can adapt to any style that may be called for during the day.

37 As a complement to a good rod I have excellent banksticks. They also are home-made from hexagonal steel for strength, and grooved where the rod will rest so that the line can run freely if necessary.

38

39

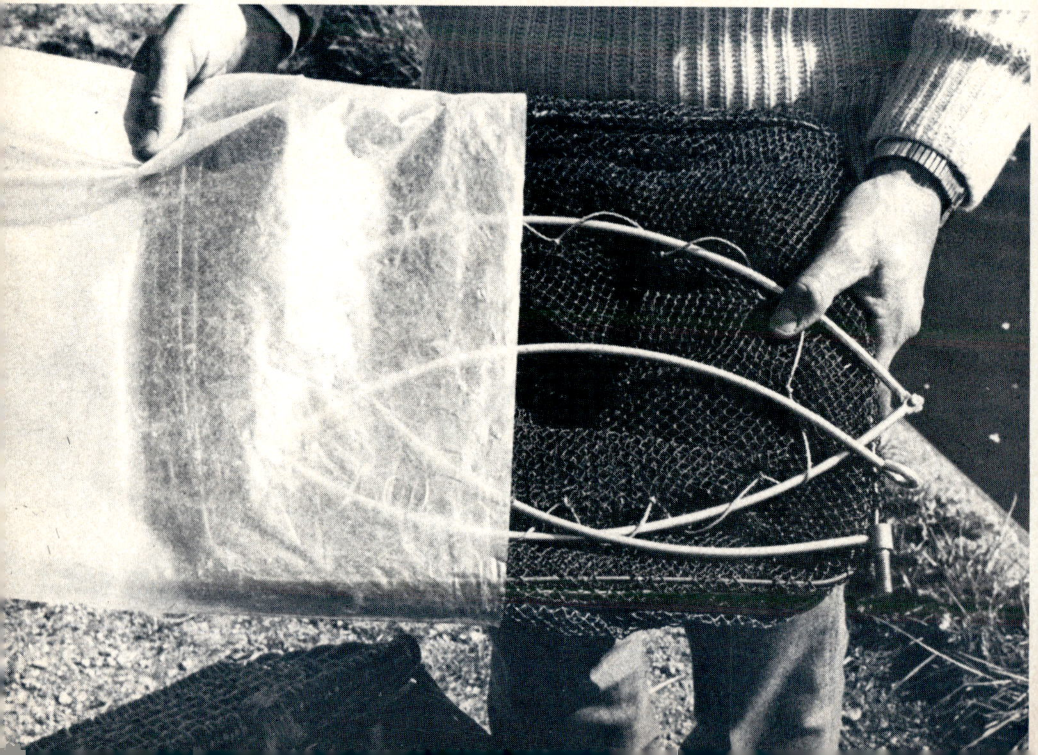

40

38 One day someone will invent a motorised basket. Until then I carry this, which contains everything I need. The following pictures show what I mean. I have made or bought every item to fit in a specific order, using every inch of space.

39 First to come out — and last in before leaving home so that it is not forgotten — is the keepnet. Circumference of the base is not so important as depth, and I examine it every time I set it up for signs of wear.

40 Hands that are wet and slimy are often cold and insensitive. Clean towels each time out are useful.

41

42

41 This slim box carries all those odds and ends that many anglers lose during the course of an outing.

42 The second tray shows clearly how everything is packed — not only to avoid rattle whilst carrying, but to prevent loss through vibration. If you have ever lost the contents of a box of shot in your bag you will know just what I mean.

43 A micro-mesh landing net is light and does not damage fish.

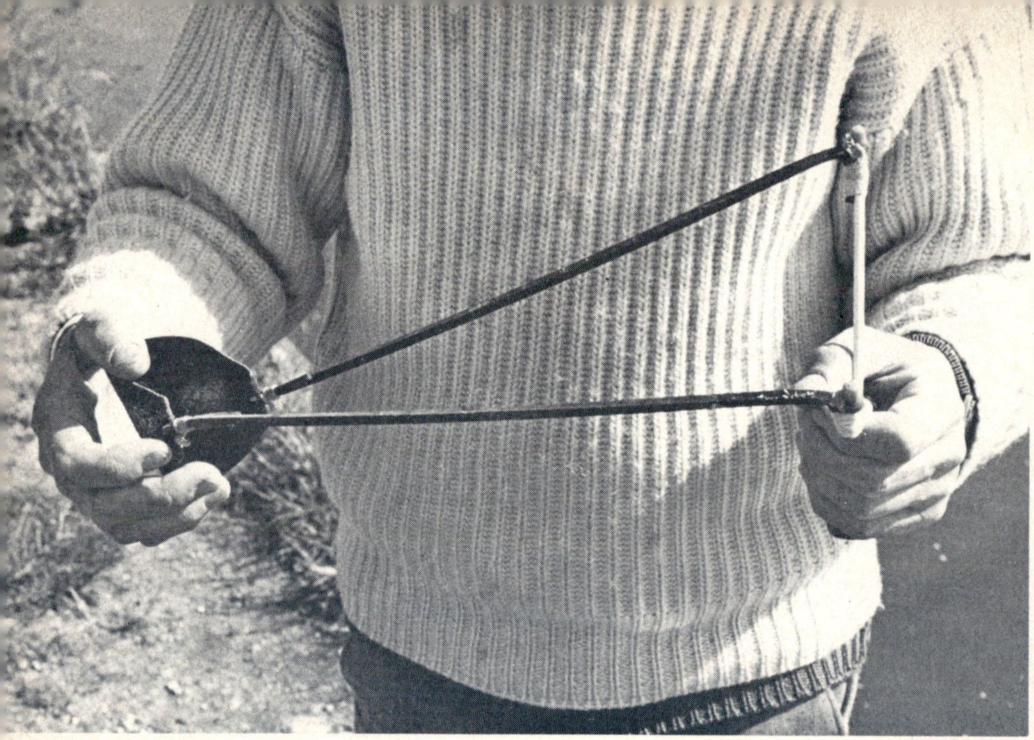

44

45

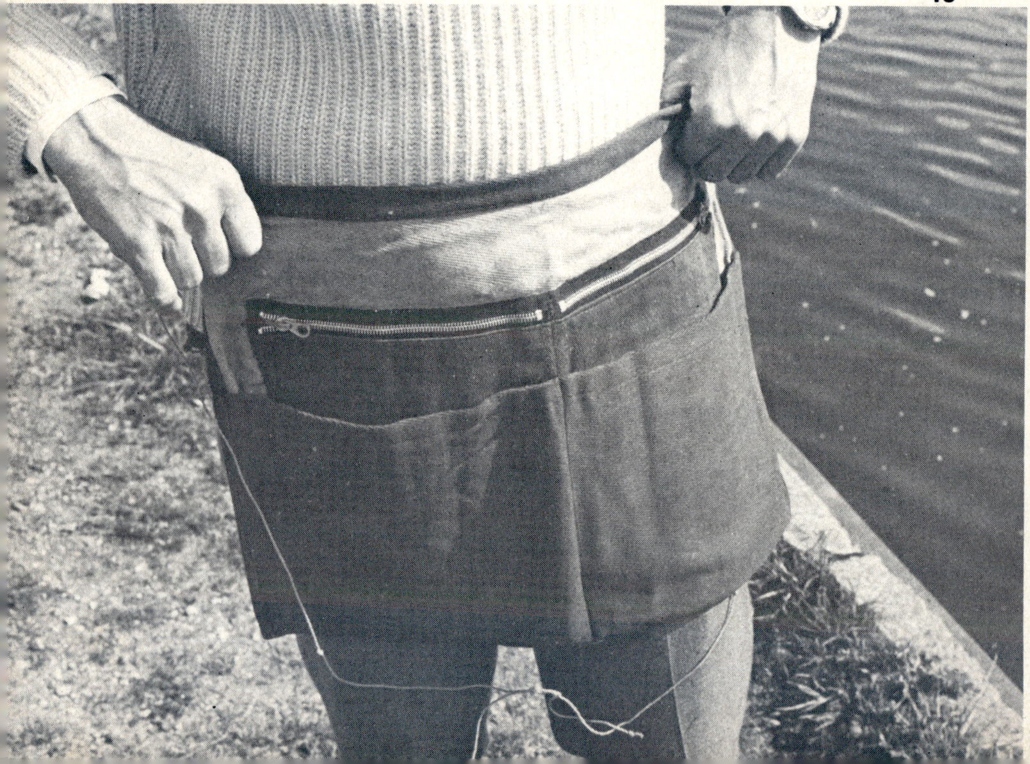

46

44 Another home-made item, a catapult with a large, strong leather cup.

45 Not to keep your clothes clean, but a very convenient way of carrying ground and hookbaits — especially maggots — during the match. This apron costs very little, and takes up little room.

46 Reels are always cleaned and checked after a match ready for the next outing. By keeping them in their cases I know that grit and dirt cannot impair their action.

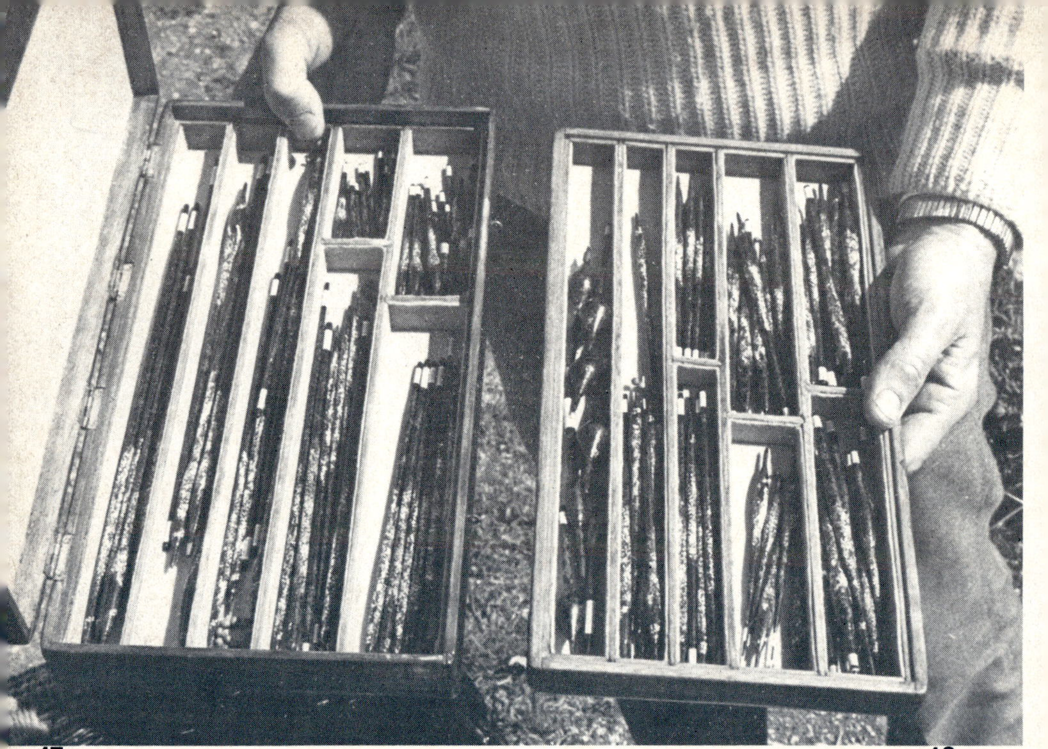

47

48

47 The floats I carry are sorted into compartments, and marked with the number of shot they will require at the base.

48 All the end gear for my roachpoles is pre-tied, floats are weighted, and winders colour-coded so that I can pick up and tie on a complete rig within minutes.

49 Again to save time, all my hook lengths are ready tied, and mounted on these home-made winders so that if I lose a ledger or trotting rig, it can be replaced within seconds.

50

51

52

50 Good waterproofs can be folded, and will be ready for use in minutes. Remember that a cold or wet matchman will be less likely to concentrate than one who is warm and dry.

51 Block end feeders in three sizes, with plenty of spares for losses.

52 If you are worried about sliding off your seat, or sitting uncomfortably during a match you cannot concentrate properly — this little trowel ensures that my basket will be set level.

53

54

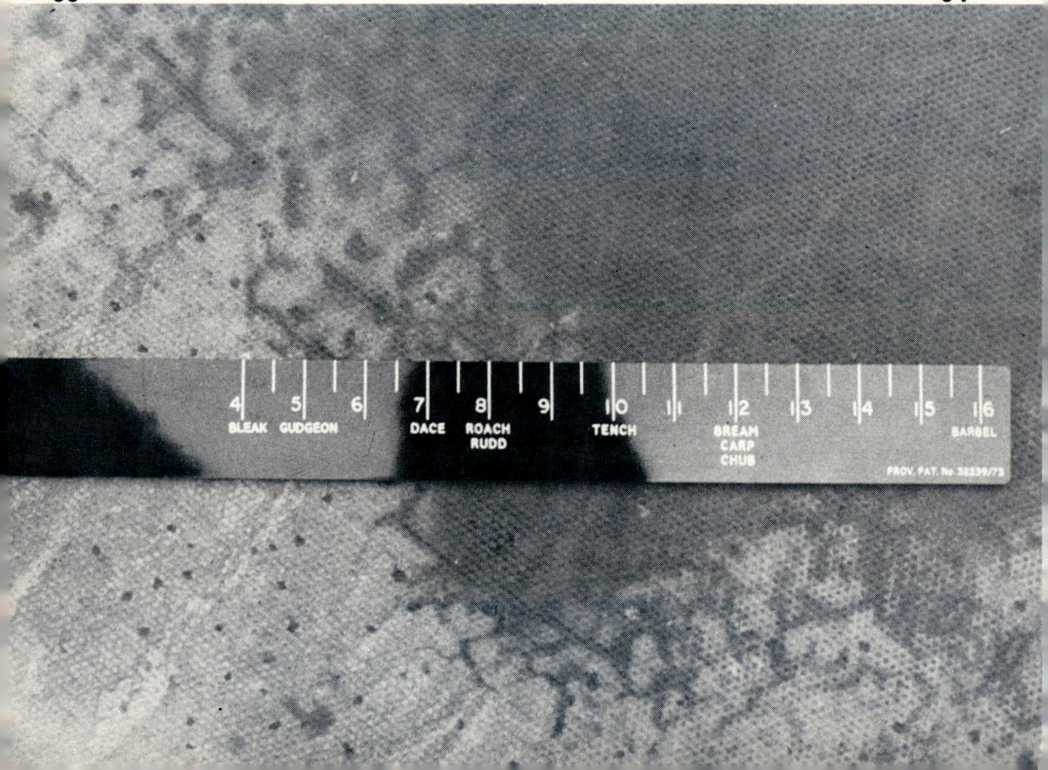
4 5 6 7 8 9 10 11 12 13 14 15 16
BLEAK
GUDGEON
DACE
ROACH
RUDD
TENCH
BREAM
CARP
CHUB
BARBEL
PROV. PAT. No 32239/73

53 Often I have to stand whilst I fish, and this home-made maggot stand stops me having to bend down and pick up maggots — a great time saver.

54 If you are fishing to size limits — this is important.

55 Here is a lay-out of all the items carried in that one basket.

56

57

58

56 I own some centrepin reels, but mostly use fixed spool models, in various sizes to suit the type of fishing I expect to do.

57 Maximum casting distance can only be obtained by filling the spool of each reel to the fullest extent.

58 I never use the slipping clutch mechanism, but prefer to screw the clutch tight and play a big fish from the handle.

BAYER
PERLON
PLATIL
Berkley
Trilene
XL
A NEW STANDARD
OF EXCELLENCE FOR
MONOFILAMENT LINE

59 60

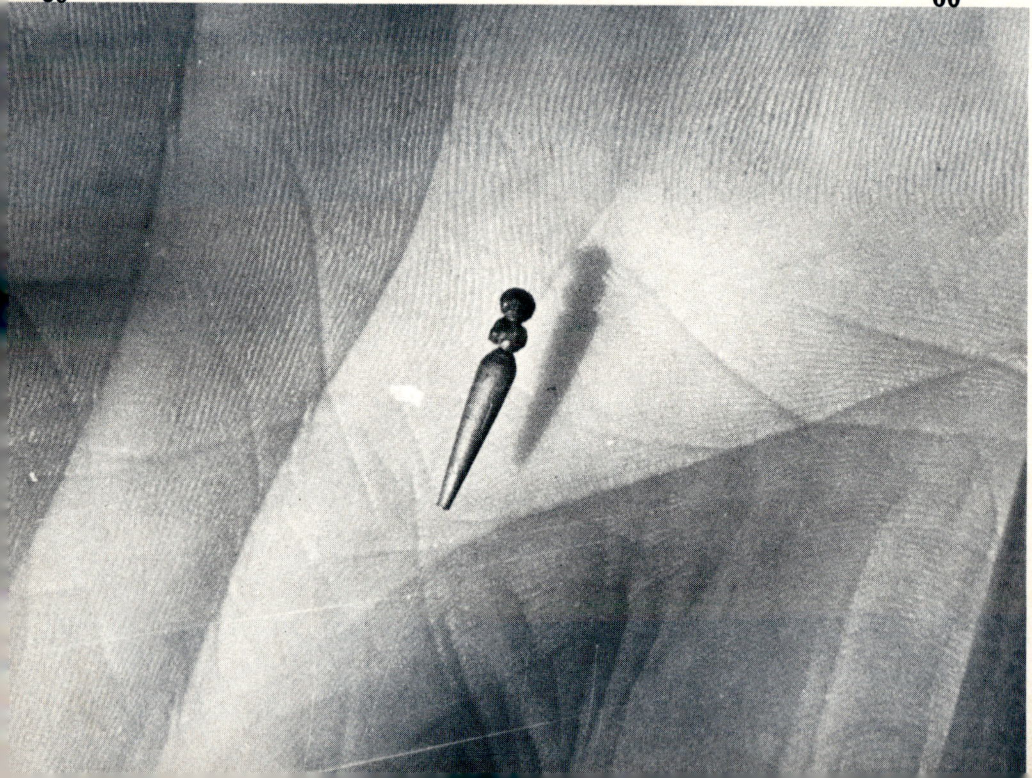

59 Some of the lines I use, in all sizes. They are kept away from strong sunlight — which can weaken them — at all times.

60 Mouse-dropping weights, sized up to the various floats, streamline my tackle and are a necessary item.

61 Obviously the match fisherman needs a wide range of hooks. Mine are all spade ends, and none of them is offset.

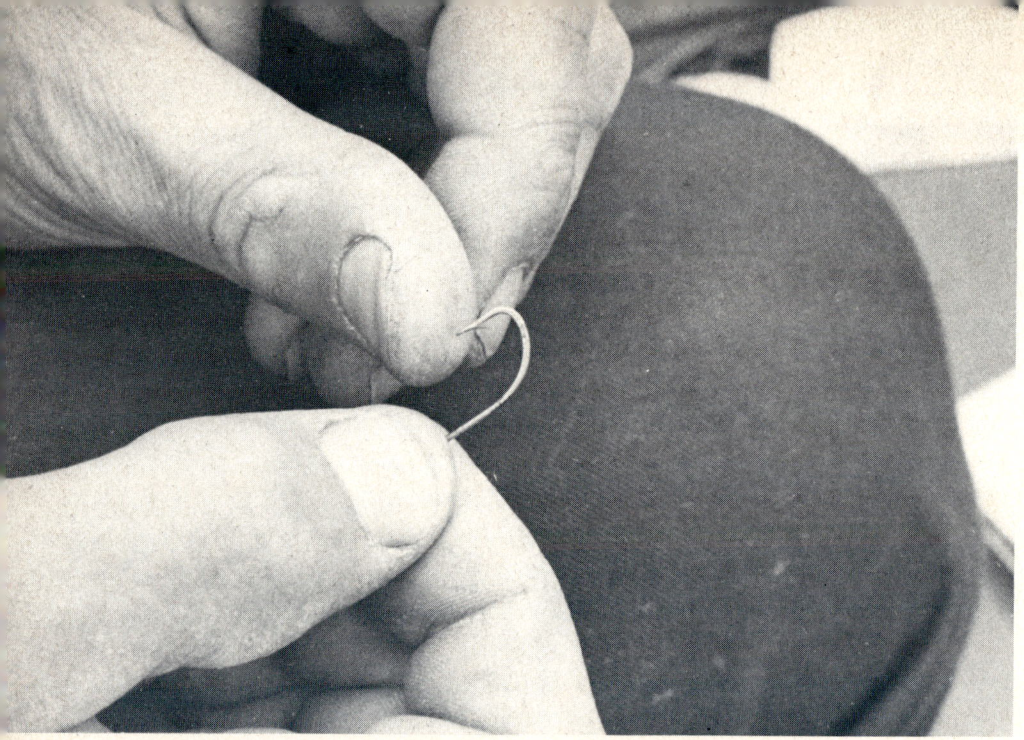

62

63

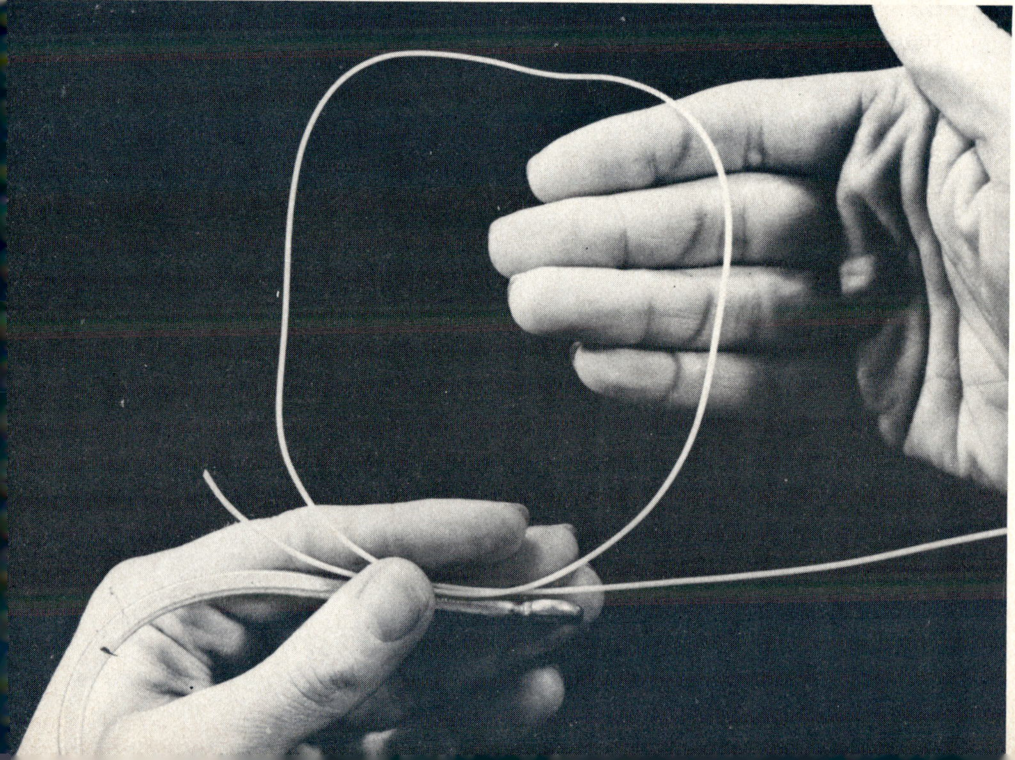

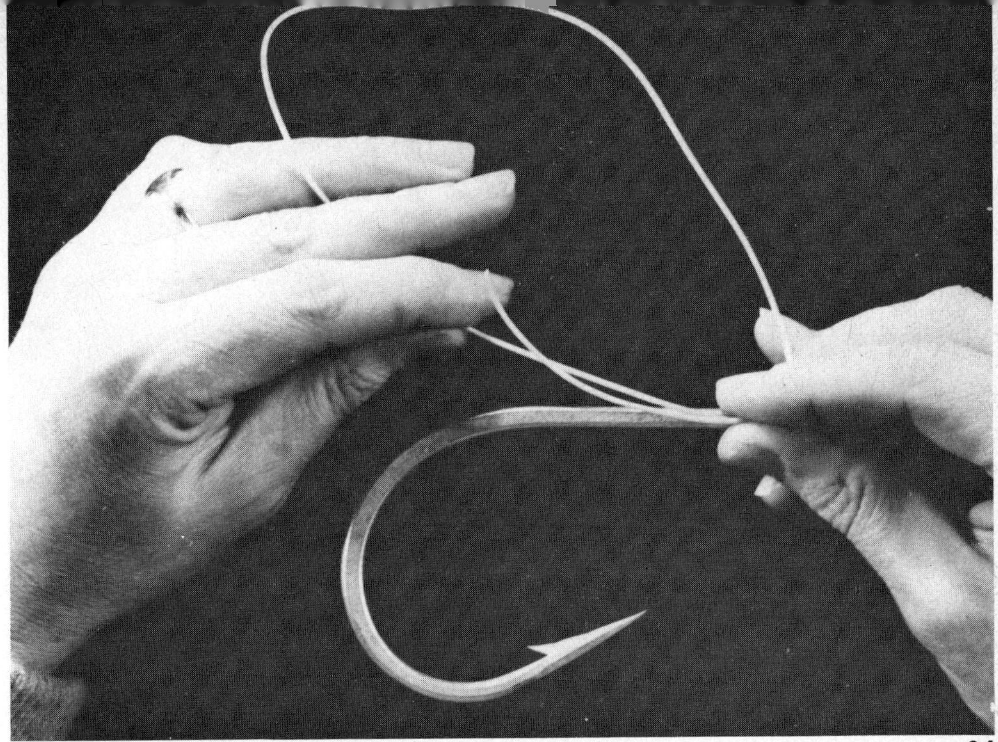

64

62 The most important thing is to test each hook before it is used; two seconds' work that can perhaps save losing a good fish.

63 This is the knot I use to tie my hooks. Make a large loop in the end of the line and place it along the shank of the hook.

64 Take the side of the loop nearest the end of the hook in the fingers of the left hand, holding the hook firmly by the spade end in the right hand.

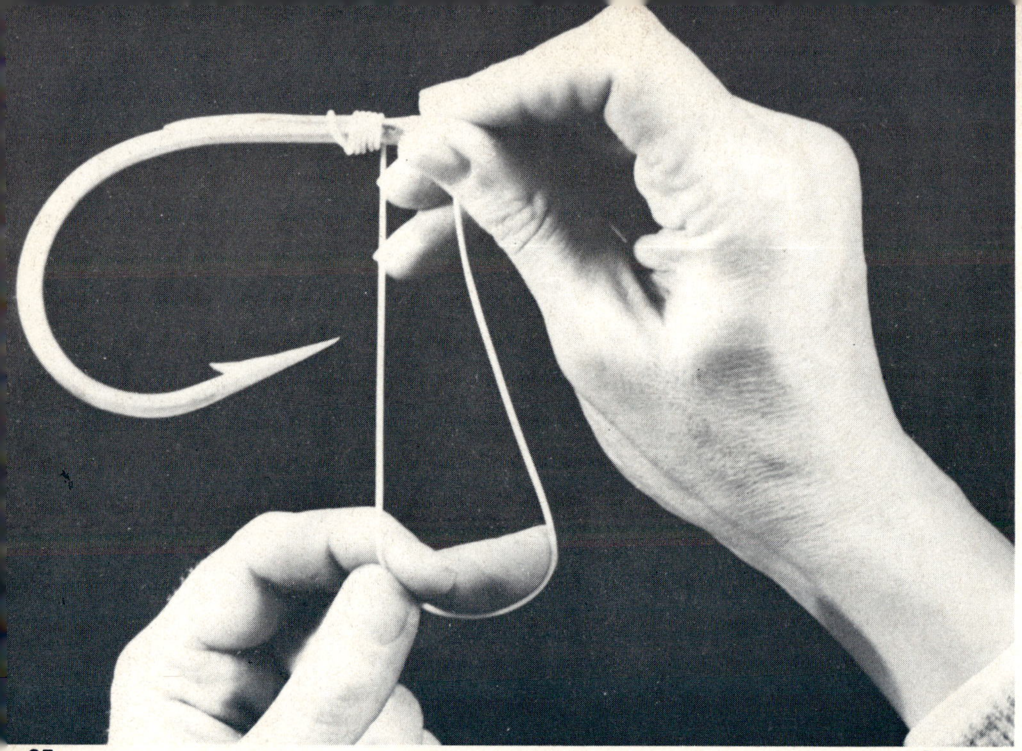

65

66

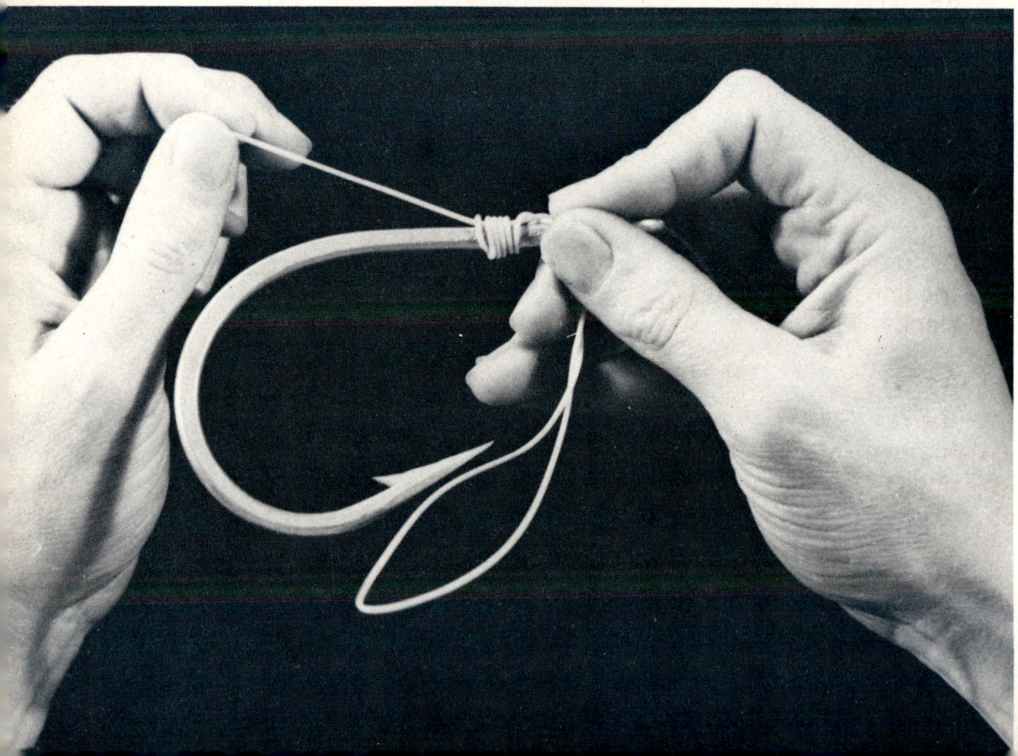

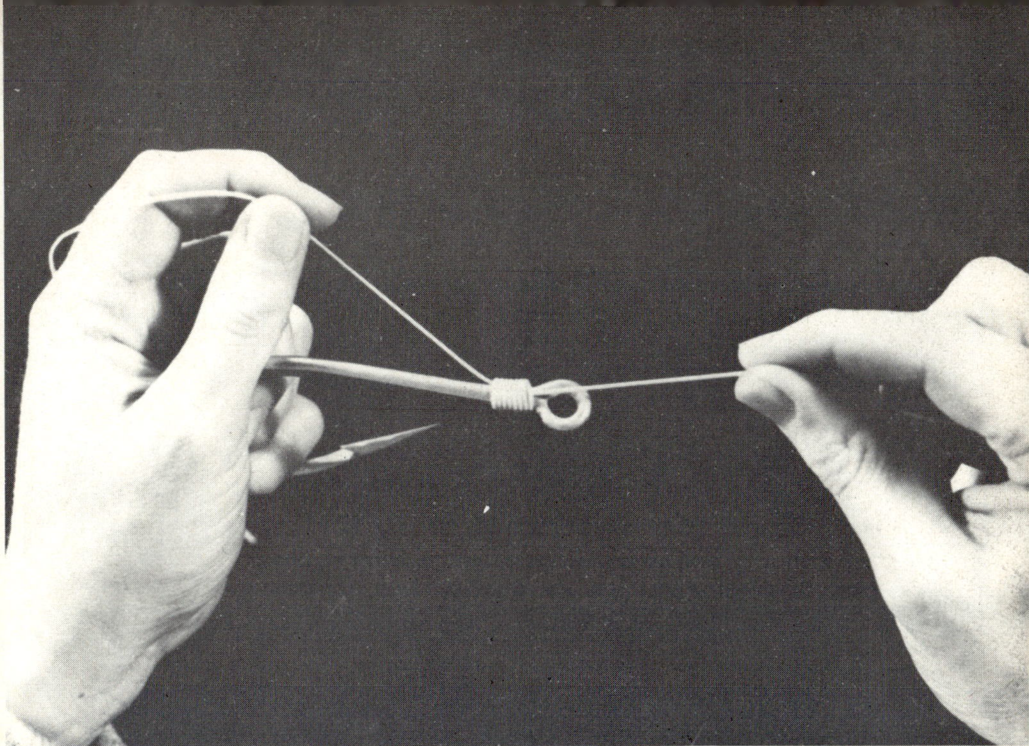

65 Wind the side of the loop in the left hand around the shank of the hook and the end of the line together, working towards the spade end, for some six turns.

66 Having achieved this, the fingers of the right hand are used to control the loop while the end of the line is pulled to remove the slack in the loop.

67 Tighten firmly and make sure the reel line comes off the shank at the back of the spade. Cut off the end.

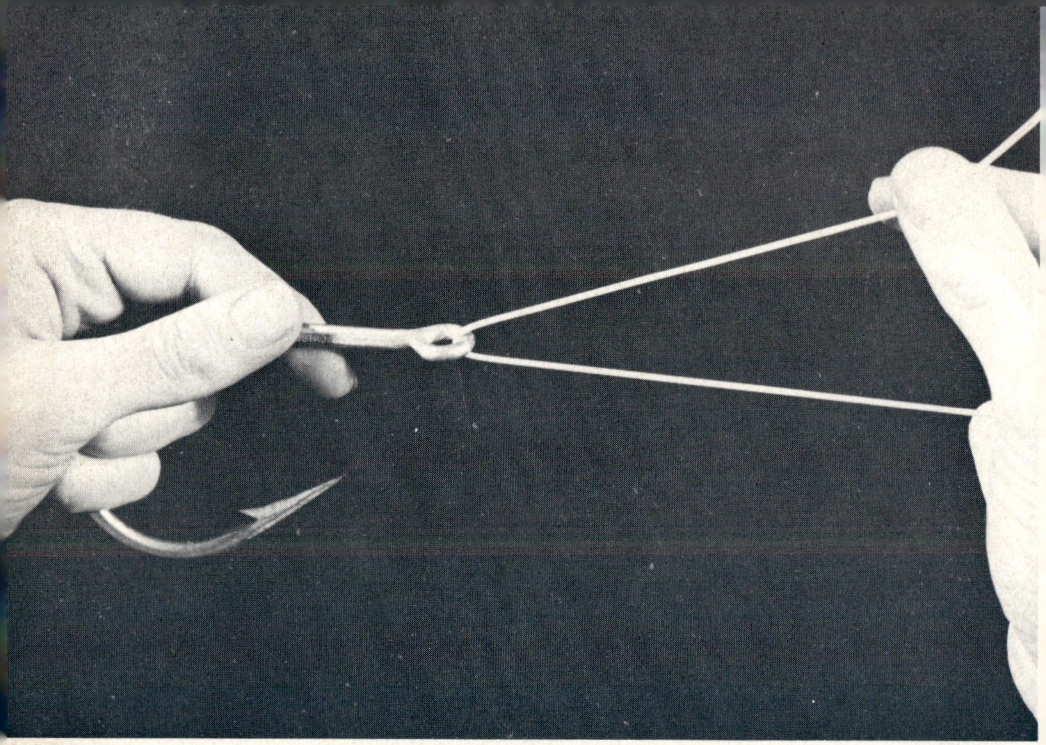

68

69

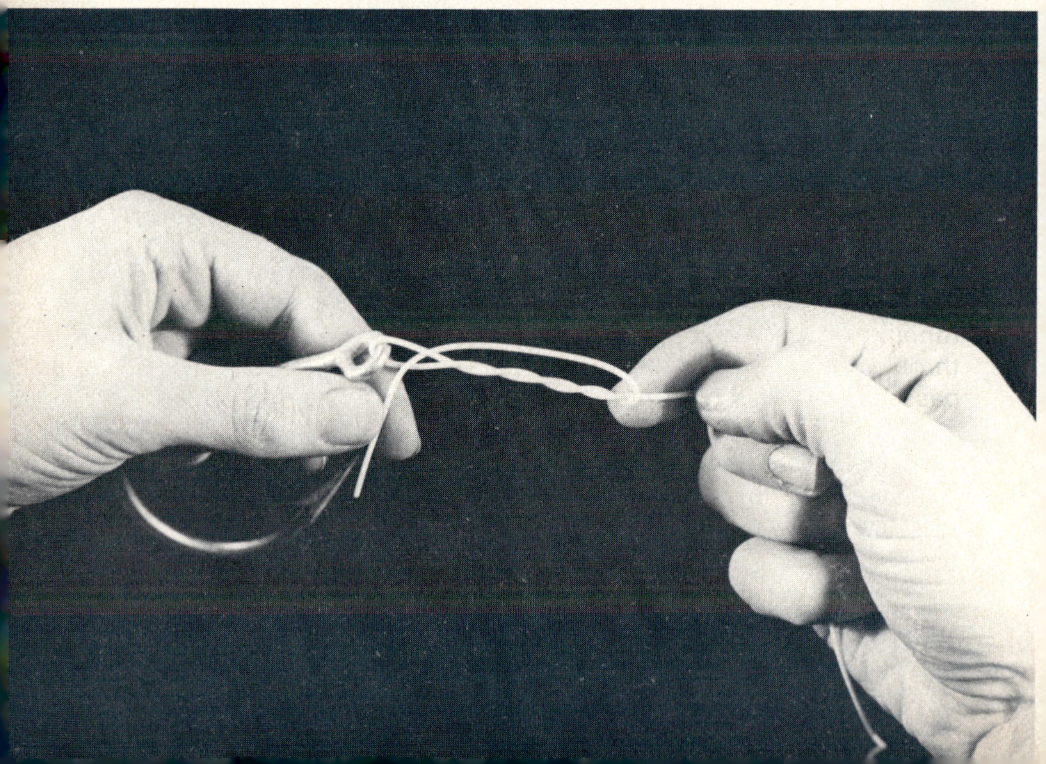

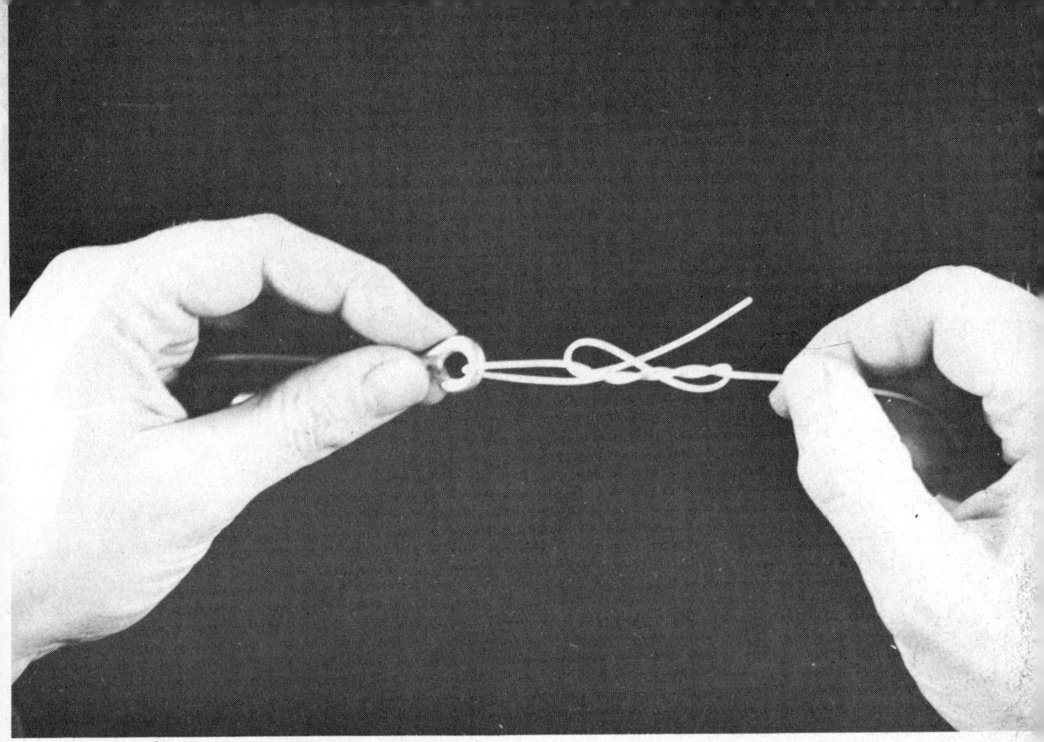

70

68 For those who like to use an eyed hook, or when tying line to a swivel, try this knot. First pass line through the metal loop.

69 Twist five or six times, then pass the end through the loop formed by the twist.

70 This action makes a loop running alongside the twist through which the end is now passed.

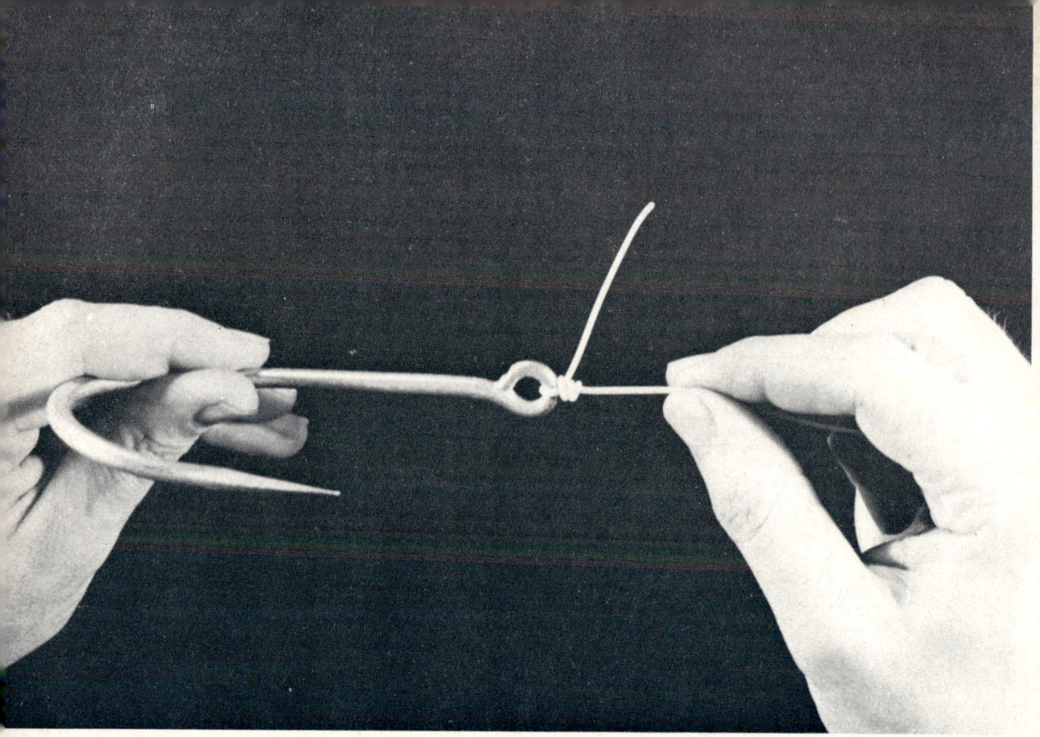

71

72

71 Moisten the knot and draw tight, assisting the knot to close with finger tips if necessary. Trim the end.

72 This round landing net is capable of handling big fish . . .

73 It is used with a long handle, making sure that I can reach from a high bank if necessary. I cut down a roachpole to make this handle, an expensive but necessary action.

74

75

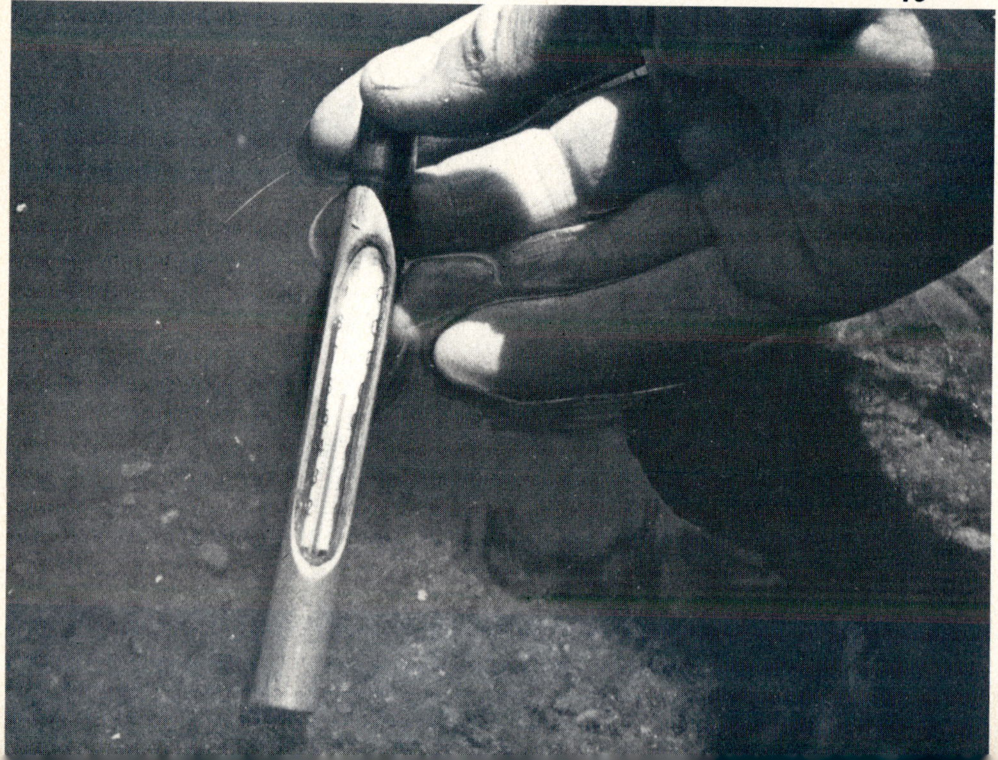

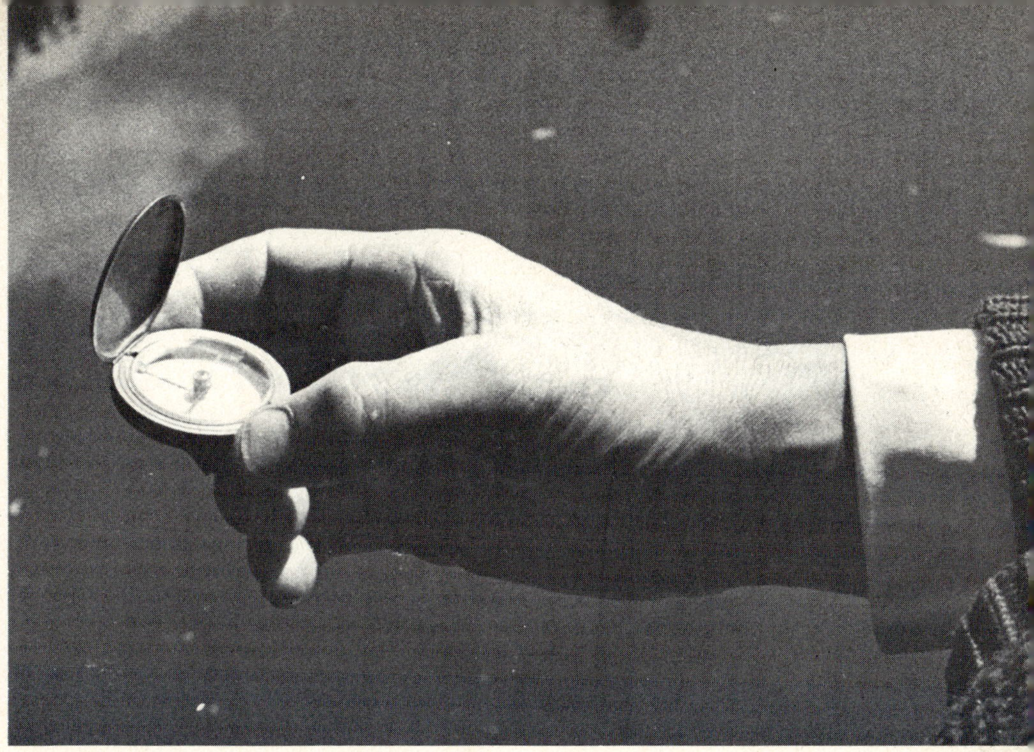

76

74 Yet another check to ensure that there are no faults in my keepnet before it is put into the water.

75 Used, and not carried. This thermometer gives me some indication of how the fish will be feeding. Or, if you prefer, it will tell me that the colder it is, the fewer fish will be required to win the match.

76 The compass is an insurance against the future. A few notes at the end of the day in a book on weather, wind direction, feeding habits can help with a future match. I am sure of my own, and the wind's position with this small aid.

77

78

77 All set in position to fish — a view from the right.

78 And the same thing, viewed this time from the left, showing everything in its right position, where I will be able to reach for it automatically.

79 One last aid to the matchman — the umbrella. Make sure it is firmly fastened into the ground, and pegged securely.

80

81

82

80 Groundbait blended at home the night before is carried in a mixing bowl, inside a large canvas bucket.

81 Final preparation, mixing with water, is done at the bank. The mix is kept firm for ease of casting.

82 A crucial moment. The groundbait must land in your swim, not in the downstream one. Practice, and a little common sense in allowing for strength of current, will pay off.

83

84

83 Naturally the float that will be used can only be decided on the day, when you have seen the water. All my floats are finely camouflaged.

84 One of several plummets carried, to allow for possible loss. This is an important moment — the plummet will tell me the depth of the water and what the swim is like on the bottom — you will feel the knock of lead on gravel, and the dull thud of mud.

85 Casting. So important — but so easy. First, allow a length of line to hang from the rod tip equal to the length of the rod.

86 Swing the rod backwards and allow the end tackle to sweep behind your shoulder.

87 Now drive it forward hard, releasing the line from the reel at the same moment. Keep the rod up to allow the line to run through. It is all done in one rhythmic swing. This needs constant practice if perfection is to be obtained.

89

88 Here is a close-up of my hands on the rod handle during the cast. It is important to keep control of the rod tip. This is where the action will finally come from.

89 Whilst trotting down, my hand is at this position on the rod handle, with the fingers controlling the line ready for an instant strike.

91

90 Throughout the passage of my float through the swim, the rod tip will cover, and control it.

91 Mending the line when it precedes the float can be done by raising the rod and then swinging the line back upstream.

93

92 If I am sitting down, the bait boxes are arranged so that I can reach a fresh maggot for hookbait, or bunch of maggots for groundbait within seconds.

93 Sometimes I have to stand, although there is always the risk that fish will be put down by my movements.

94

95

96

94 Here the maggot stand comes into its own, saving not only my back muscles, but valuable seconds when I rebait.

95 I always carry a good supply of pinkies for groundbait.

96 If I am fishing near the bank, I can feed the swim by throwing in loose pinkies.

97

98

97 Further out the catapult has to be used — but one must be prepared for the bait to 'spread' more with this method.

98 Playing a fish from the reel. Remember to keep in touch with the fish and not to try to force the issue. The loss of a big one can cost the contest.

99 Small fish can be played from the line, and landed with the minimum of time wasted.

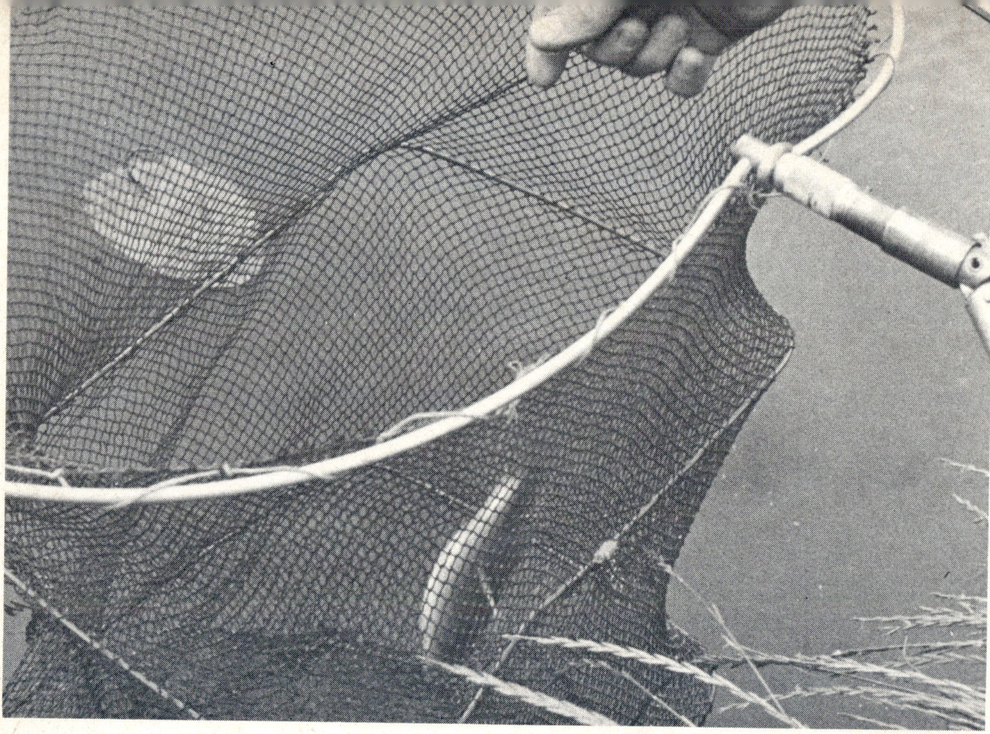

100

101

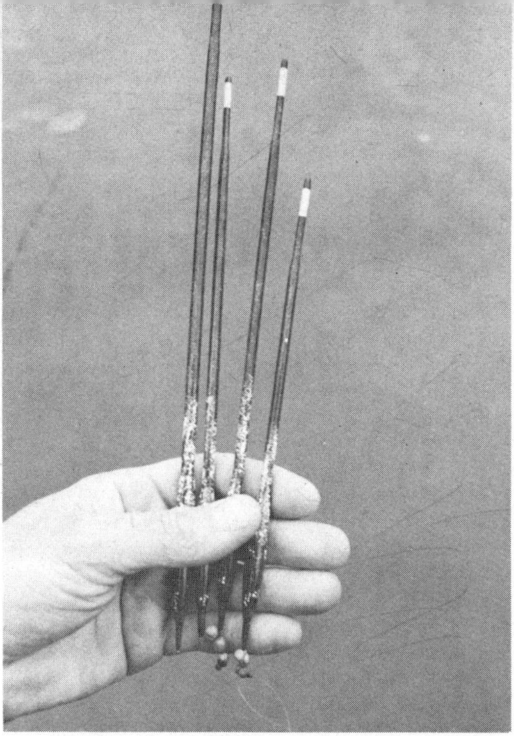

102

103

100 Small fish should be out, in the keepnet, and the hook back in the water, practically in one movement.

101 The advantage of a large mouth to the keepnet — if a fish should drop, it won't escape.

102 Home-made zoomers. Use the smallest one necessary to reach the swim you intend to fish.

103 Remember that less effort is required to cast a heavy zoomer than to get a small float into the same position. It is easy to overcast your distance.

104

105

106

104 Laying-on. A deadly method where the current will allow. Here the rod rests are set into position so that I can have control over the rod.

105 This is the ideal float and rod tip position — one small movement from the float, and there is so little line that a very small strike will immediately drive the hook home.

106 Ledgering. Not a lazy way of catching big fish — it's every bit as delicate and demanding as float fishing. Perhaps the only way it differs in delicacy is in the strike — shown here.

107 Quiver and swing tips. I use both — swing tips for still waters, quiver tips for running water of any strength.

108 Correct position for swing tip ledgering, with the rod tip low, the swing tip at an acute angle, showing the slightest movement.

108

109

109 Ready to strike — hand on the rod, little finger controlling the reel housing.

110 Target boards and rod rests are very important when using a quiver tip. Make sure the board is large, and clearly painted. Strong rod rests are necessary to give firm support to the rod.

111

112

111 These are the rod rest ends I prefer, holding the rod still but allowing the line to run if necessary.

112 Of course the rod rests and target board should be in line. Several attempts may be necessary before a dead sighting down the rod and onto the board is obtained.

113 The final picture — angler at an angle to the river, rod and rests in a progressive downward line onto the target board.

114 This is where the work in pre-tying my hook links pays off. I can change one within seconds.

115 This picture shows how they are actually held in place with a pin so that they can be released quickly.

116

117

118

116 Ledger leads. Carried in many sizes, and, where a swivel is used, given a little drop of oil to make sure they turn smoothly.

117 To my mind, the best model of a block end feeder. Easily stopped with a patent line stop, or a small split shot.

118 If your groundbait for the block end is not stiff, the cast leaves a trail.

119

120

119 Casting a ledger. Stage one — leave enough line from the rod tip to give 'swing' during the cast.

120 Swing the rig forward . . .

121 . . . then backwards.

122

122 Bring it overhead with an easy swing, and release the line. Never attempt to 'force' the cast.

123

123 If I am going to use the roachpole, I always have one or two others set up so that I can cover the fish. If they move out — I just swap my pole for a longer one.

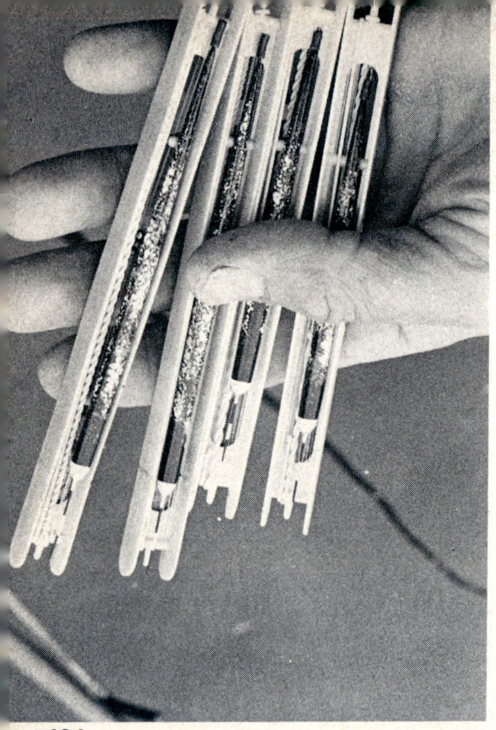

124 My end gear for use with poles is ready wound, and the winders they are wound onto are colour coded so that I save time. Three colours are enough to cover light, medium and heavy rigs.

125 Here is one way of attaching the rig to a pole. Simply loop through the eyed end.

126 Here's another way. First a light alloy tube is screwed into the end of the pole.

127 Into a slotted groove at the end of this tube can be looped a short length of round elastic, and onto this the line can be tied. There is a 'buffering' effect at the strike, and this saves a break when using a very light line.

124

125

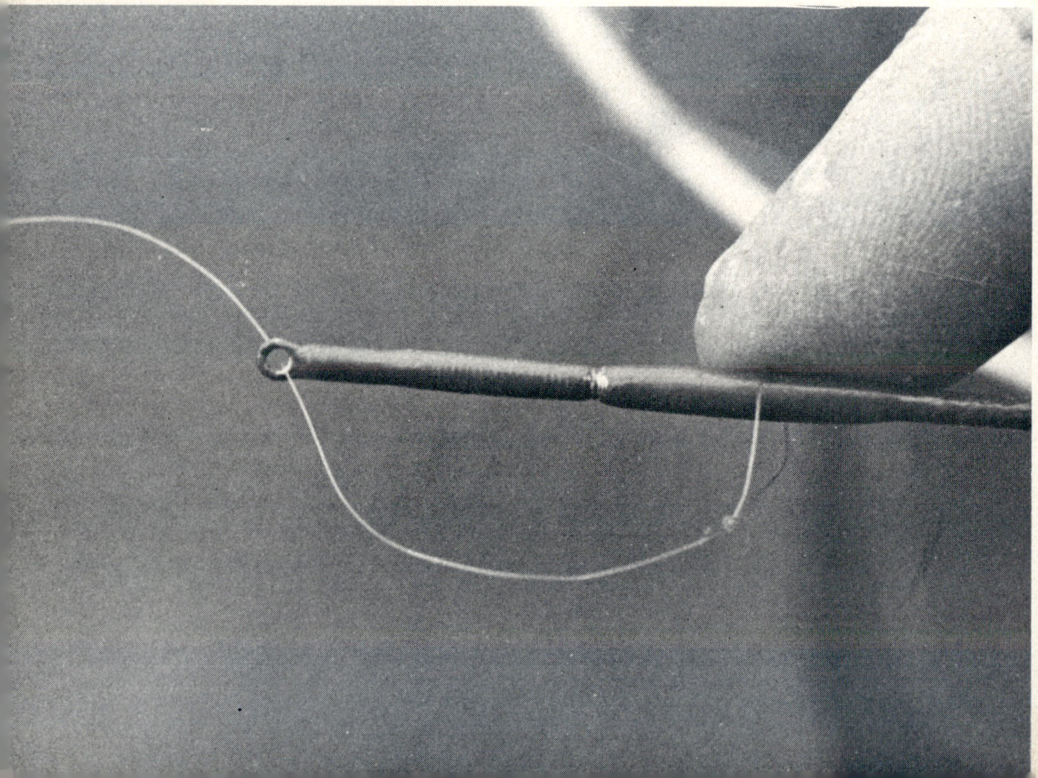

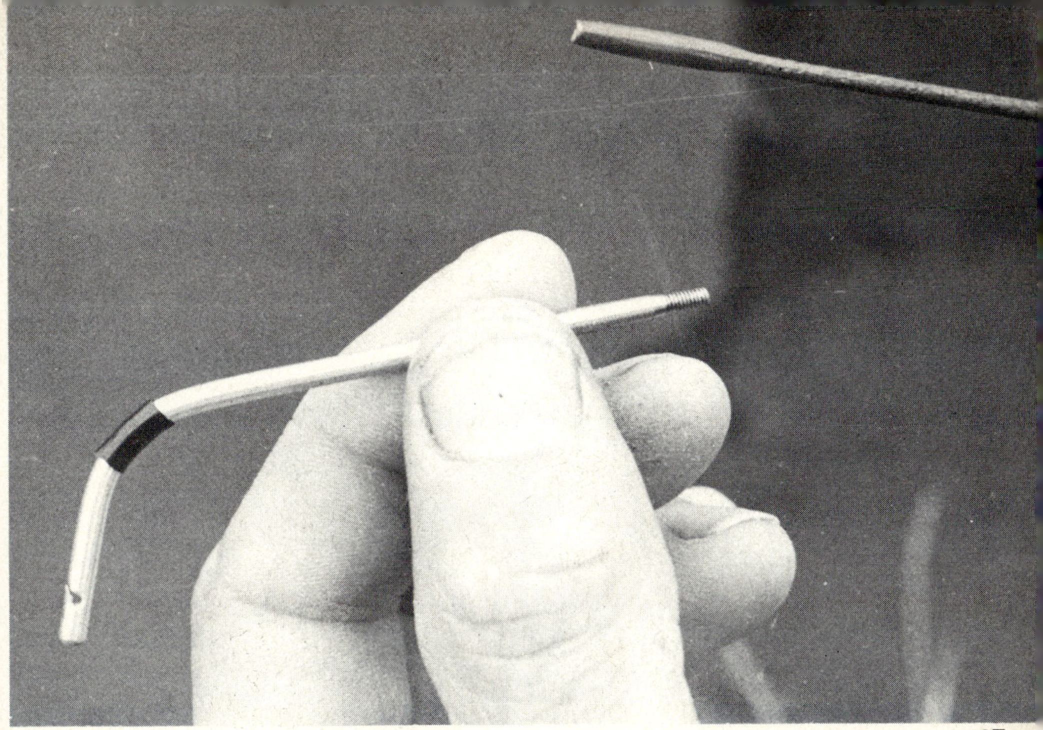

126

127

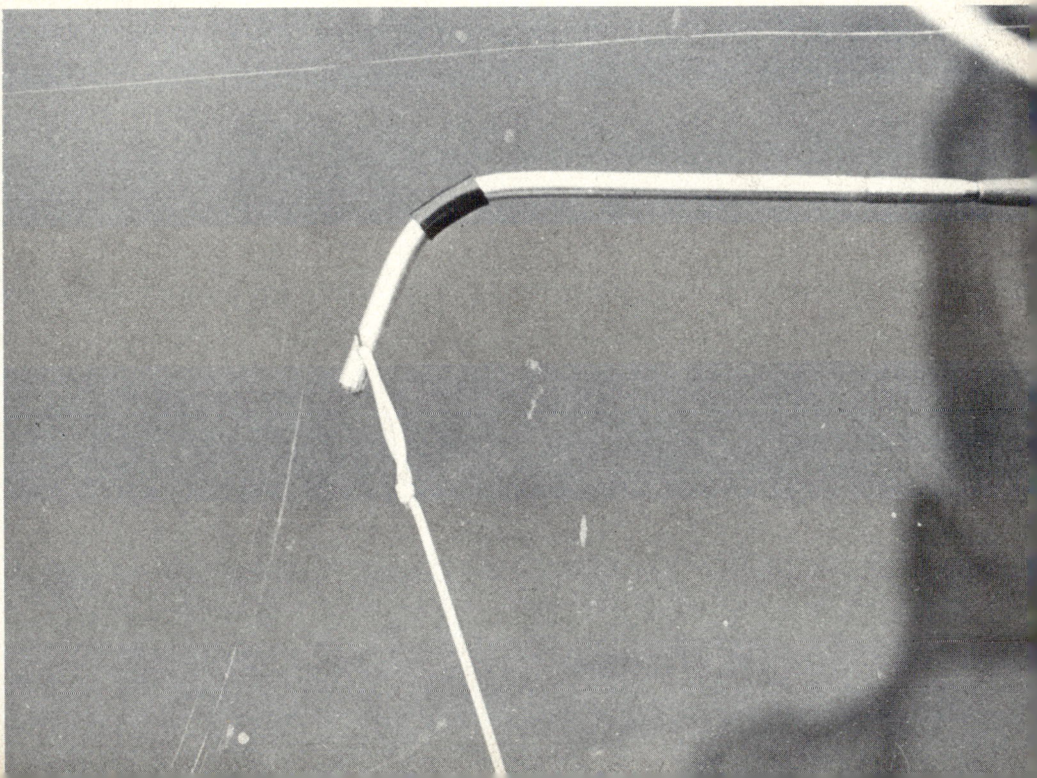

128

129

130

128 Holding a small roachpole. Using the knee takes the weight off the wrist, and leaves me free to strike quickly.

129 Two hands are needed for a long pole, and the strike comes from the forward hand when a bite is recorded.

130 Here is an important point overlooked by many pole anglers. The tip of the pole must cover the float all the time — this is the whole object of using a pole. There is so little loose line that the strike and actual hooking come at the same time.

131

132

131 If I have good fish feeding near the bottom, and small fish on the surface, I take care to feed only the bigger fish by lowering the groundbait onto the bed with a bait layer.

132 Once hooked, a fish should be played immediately out of the swim water, to avoid disturbing the rest of the shoal.

133 If the fish is large, the butt of the pole must be unshipped to land it. Never attempt to lift a large fish out. Not only will you lose him, but time will be wasted in tying on another hook.

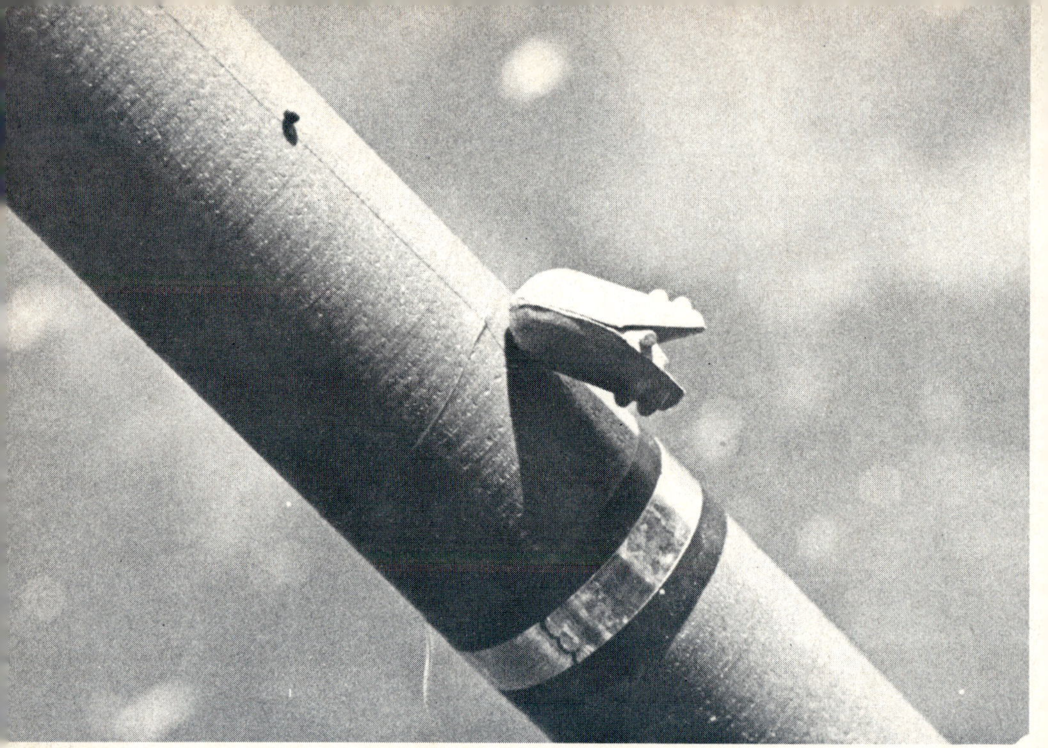

134

135

136

134 To avoid loose tackle getting caught up I clip a small plummet onto the hook and half-hitch the line around the base of each roach-pole when it is not in use.

135 If there is not room to lay a pole down behind me, this spike will enable me to stand it vertically in the ground.

136 Many people worry about the presence of boats going through the swim when they are fishing a match. Believe me, boats have been using rivers for years, and fish are quite used to them.

138

137 Of course, much of what I have written so far applies to still water as well as rivers.

138 If you are float fishing in still water, it is most important to 'bully' a fish out of the swim. Otherwise the rest will soon be frightened off.

140

139 Play him right into the bank, at your side, and land him from this position.

140 Remember always to play the fish over the net, and then lift it. Never stab at the fish with the net.

139

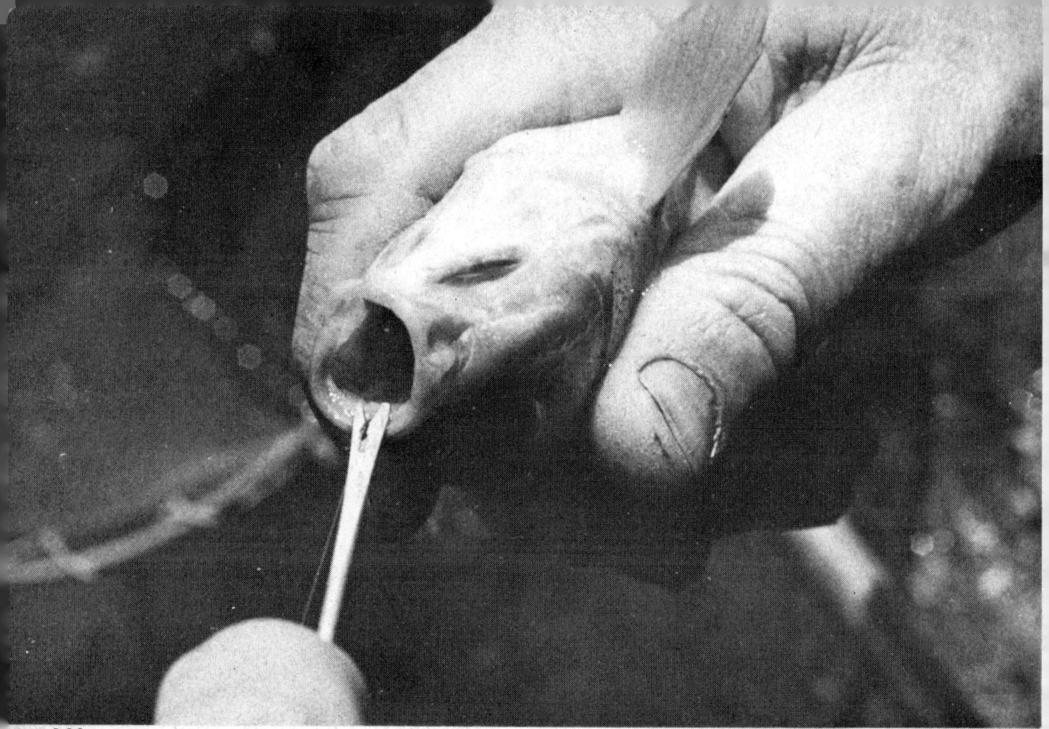

141

141 Disgorging takes time — but be careful. If you break the hook, more time will be wasted in tying another one on.

142 I have tried to tell you the secret of successful match fishing in this book. There are no gimmicks, no short cuts, no special tackle, no frills or fancies. Successful match fishing is just careful preparation, hard work, and then, if things are not going too well, further checking and a lot more work on some small detail. If you don't believe me, start at the front of the book again, and see just how many of the jobs I do are those which *you* do before, during, or after a match. Good luck!

142